The Moral Foundations of Life

Oswald Chambers' Publications—

APPROVED UNTO GOD
BAFFLED TO FIGHT BETTER
BIBLICAL ETHICS
BIBLICAL PSYCHOLOGY
BRINGING SONS UNTO GLORY
CALLED OF GOD
CHRISTIAN DISCIPLINE, VOLS. 1 AND 2
CONFORMED TO HIS IMAGE
DISCIPLES INDEED
GOD'S WORKMANSHIP
HE SHALL GLORIFY ME
IF THOU WILT BE PERFECT
IF YE SHALL ASK
KNOCKING AT GOD'S DOOR
MY UTMOST FOR HIS HIGHEST
NOT KNOWING WHITHER
OUR BRILLIANT HERITAGE
OUR PORTRAIT IN GENESIS
RUN TODAY'S RACE
SHADE OF HIS HAND
SO SEND I YOU
STILL HIGHER FOR THE HIGHEST
STUDIES IN THE SERMON ON THE MOUNT
THE HIGHEST GOOD
THE LOVE OF GOD
THE MORAL FOUNDATIONS OF LIFE
THE PHILOSOPHY OF SIN
THE PLACE OF HELP
THE PSYCHOLOGY OF REDEMPTION
THE SERVANT AS HIS LORD
THE SHADOW OF AN AGONY
WORKMEN OF GOD

———

OSWALD CHAMBERS: AN UNBRIBED SOUL

The Moral Foundations of Life

A Series of Talks on the Ethical
Principles of the Christian Life

Oswald Chambers

OSWALD CHAMBERS PUBLICATIONS
ASSOCIATION

and

CHRISTIAN LITERATURE CRUSADE
Fort Washinton, Pennsylvania 19034

CHRISTIAN LITERATURE CRUSADE
FORT WASHINGTON
PENNSYLVANIA 19034

MARSHALL, MORGAN & SCOTT
116 BAKER STREET
LONDON W1M 2BB

This edition (paperback) 1975

Printed photolitho in Great Britain by J. W. Arrowsmith Ltd., Bristol

CONTENTS

FOREWORD

I SEE sometimes in London the preparations being made for the sure foundations of one of the great modern buildings to be erected there. Far below the surface-level men and machines toil patiently on work which soon will be hidden, but which alone will make the towering building secure. These Talks on Moral Foundations take us to that depth below the surface of our everyday life where the foundations are laid for enduring sainthood. They deal profoundly with such matters as Habit, Thinking, the Will, Behaviour. The subject of Christian ethical obligation is of paramount importance in the thought life of to-day. The very basis of our religion, our moral and spiritual standing, is being challenged. Here will be found a valiant answer to the secular, sceptical and lawless questionings of our time.

The writer was one of God's saints ; and also one of those sane Christian thinkers who see into the deep places of our strange, perplexing yet alluring human life. Already the chapters have proved their worth as articles in the *B.T.C. Journal*. Now in this compact form they will serve for hours of instruction in righteousness as they illumine these dim regions of the soul in the blazing light of Holy Scripture.

D. L.

THE WILL IN DISCIPLESHIP

Luke ix. 61–62.

Beware of thinking of will as a faculty. Will simply means the whole nature active. We talk about people having a weak will or a strong will, it is a misleading idea. When we speak of a man having a weak will, we mean he is without any impelling passion, he is the creature of every dominating influence; with good people he is good, with bad people he is bad, not because he is a hypocrite, but because he has no ruling passion, and any strong personality knits him into shape. Will is the essential element in God's creation of a man. I cannot *give up* my will: I must exercise it.

The Want To.

"Lord, I will follow Thee;"

Want is a conscious tendency towards a particular end. My wants take shape when something awakens my personal life. An invalid if left alone has no wants, he wants neither to live nor to die; but when he sees a person full of bounding physical health, a want to be like him is instantly awakened. Whatever awakens my person awakens a want. In this incident the presence of Jesus awakened a conscious want to follow Him, a want to be like Him.

9

(a) *The Want in Conscience.* The first appeal was to conscience, and could be expressed in this way: 'Follow Him, He is Thy supreme Lord.' The presentation of Jesus Christ always awakens that desire, the presentation of abstract ideals never does. You can present morality, good principles, the duty of loving your neighbour, and never arouse a man's conscience to want anything; but when you present Jesus Christ, instantly there is a dumb awakening; a want to be what He would like me to be. It is not conviction of sin, but an awakening out of the sleep of indifference into a want.

There are some things that are without meaning for us. For instance, to be told that God will give us the Holy Spirit if we ask Him, may be a dead proposition; but when we come in contact with a person filled with the Spirit of God we instantly awaken to a want. Or again, if you tell half a dozen clean-living, upright, sterling men that God so loved them that He gave His Son to die for them, only their good breeding will keep them from being amused—'Why should Jesus Christ die for me'? It is not a living proposition to them, not in the sphere of their life at all. Their morality is well within their own grasp, they are clean living and upright, all that can be desired; they will never be awakened in that way; but present them with Jesus Christ, or with a life that is like His life, and instantly there will awaken in them a want they were not conscious of before. That is why Jesus said, "If I had not come . . ., they had not had sin: but now they have no cloke for their sin." You can never argue anyone into the Kingdom of heaven, you cannot argue anyone anywhere. The only result of arguing is to prove to your own mind that you are right and the other fellow wrong. You cannot argue for truth; but immediately Incarnate Truth is presented, a want awakens in the soul which only God can meet. Conscience is that faculty of the spirit which fits itself on to the highest a man knows; and when the light of Jesus Christ is thrown on what is regarded as the highest, conscience records exactly and the reason is startled and amazed (cf. Acts xxvi. 9).

(b) *The Want in Heart*. The presence of Jesus awakened a want in this man's heart. Heart is the centre of all the vital activities of body, soul and spirit. Never think of the heart in the way the old psychology thought of the will, viz., as a compartment, a kind of hat-box into which you put all your convictions and dole them out occasionally when you lift the lid. The heart is the centre of a man's personality. "For out of the heart proceed . . .," said our Lord. You can never tell from a man's life to date what he is going to want next, because the real element of want is not logical. A man's reasoning is based on something more than reason, there is always an incalculable element.

(c) *The Want in Desire*. The want in conscience and in heart urges a man to immediate action: "Lord, I will follow Thee." It was the finest, profoundest element in the man that made him say it. In his conscience, in the deep depths of his personality, there was awakened the desire to follow Jesus and to be like Him. The measure of a man's want is seen in the nature of the power that awakened it. No man can stand in front of Jesus Christ and say, 'I want to make money.' He can stand before a successful commercial man and find the desire awakened in him to be like him and make money. This man was in contact with the Prince of persons, the Lord Jesus Christ, consequently the deep desire of his heart was for the very highest, 'Lord, I want to follow Thee; and I not only want to, but I will.'

"*A wish is often of an abstract character, directed towards some single element into a concrete event, without reference to accompanying circumstances.*" (*Mackenzie.*)

When I see Jesus Christ I simply want to be what He wants me to be. A wish is more definite than a want, which is inarticulate, something I am conscious of and that is all. Contact with a personality will always harden our wishing into a clear initiative along certain lines. For example, when a boy sees a soldier he wishes to be a soldier; when he sees an engineer he wishes to be an engineer, and so on. We have to select the domain of our wishes. At a time of religious awakening when Jesus Christ is in the ascendant and I come into close contact with Him, I wish to be a Christian. I have never known conviction of sin, never seen the need for the removal of the wrong disposition and identification with Jesus, but I wish to be like Him. The 'wish to' simply sees the end of the desire and takes no account of the means to that end.

(*a*) *Re-sensitised Sympathy.* Our wishes move in various domains. We cannot hold ourselves in a handful for we are never sure what is going to happen in the domain of our wishes. We may have all our wishes in a certain domain and be perfectly master of them, with everything clear and simple; then a bereavement comes, and instantly the domain of our wishing is completely altered, we are suddenly put into sensitive sympathy with things we never thought about before. When Jesus Christ is in the ascendant the wish moves in the domain in which He lives, the sensitiveness of our wishing answers to Him in a general softening of our whole nature. We are not conscious of wishing to possess any particular virtue, of wishing to be this or that; we simply wish to be in perfect sympathy with Him and His purposes. The only point of rest is for a man to have his sympathies sensitised by Jesus Christ, because the basis of our nature is always open to let us into some unsuspected 'hell' until we have been dominated by Our Lord. When Our Lord speaks of discipleship He catalogues the other loves (see Luke xiv. 26), and says that our love to Him must be the dominant love of all, because any of those other loves may be a trap-door to something entirely removed from God's purposes.

(*b*) *Reflection of Sublimity.* Abstract principles have no more power to lift a man than a man has to lift himself; but any man, no matter how sunk in sin, will answer to Jesus Christ when He is presented. To tell a man who is down and out to get up and do the right thing can never help him; but when once Jesus Christ is presented to him there is a reflected wish to be what Jesus wants him to be. It is appalling how many books and sermons there are to-day that simply present abstract truths. Jesus Christ appeals to the highest and the lowest, to the rich young ruler type of man, and to the man whom no ethics or moral principles can touch. Always keep Jesus Christ in the front; He says Himself He is to be there. "I, if I be lifted up from the earth, will draw all men unto Me."

(*c*) *Recession of Second Thought.* "Lord, I will follow Thee; but . . ."

The wish ought to be followed by immediate obedience. I must take the wish and translate it into resolution and then into action; if I don't, the wish will translate itself into a corrupting power in my life instead of a redeeming power. This principle holds good in the matter of emotions. A sentimentalist is one who delights to have high and devout emotions stirred whilst reading in an arm-chair, or in a prayer meeting, but he never translates his emotions into action. Consequently a sentimentalist is usually callous, self-centred and selfish, because the emotions he likes to have stirred do not cost him anything, and when he comes across the same things in the domain where things are real and not sentimental, the revenge comes along the line of selfishness and meanness, which is always the aftermath of an unfulfilled emotion. The higher the emotion, the purer the desire, the viler is the revenge in the moral character unless the emotion is worked out on its right level. It is better never to have seen the light, better never to wish to be what you are not than to have the desire awakened and never to have resolved it into action. Always do something along the line of the emotion that has been stirred; if you do not, it will corrupt that which was good before. The curbing of the outward action revenges itself in a meaner disposition on the inside, and the higher the religious emotion, the more appalling is the reaction unless it is worked out on its own level. There are those whose language and habits are coarse, yet they are not vile in their inner disposition, and suddenly they manifest graces and beauties of character that amaze you. They answer to the call given by Jesus Christ, while others of the Pharisee type do not answer (cf. Matthew xxi. 28-32). Jesus Christ said it was impossible for the man who is self-centred in his particular impression of himself to believe in Him (John v. 44).

THE WILL TO.

"And Jesus said unto him, no man having put his hand to the plough, and looking back, is fit for the kingdom of God."

The will to, means I must act; it is not sufficient to want to, to wish to, I must act on the wish instantly, no matter what it costs. Whenever the conviction of God's Spirit comes there is the softening of the whole nature to obey; but if the obedience is not instant there will come a metallic hardening and a corrupting of the guidance of God.

(*a*) *The Inspired Instinct.* Whenever you stand in the presence of Jesus Christ, as He is portrayed in the Scriptures and made real to you by the Holy Spirit, the instincts of your heart will always be inspired: *let them lead.* We read that when Jesus preached His first public sermon, all the people "wondered at the gracious words which proceeded out of His mouth;" their hearts were inspired as they listened to Him, their instincts turned in the right direction; then their prejudices came in the way and they closed down the witness of their hearts, broke up the service and tried to fling Him over the brow of the hill (Luke iv. 16–30). Always let the instinct that rules you in the presence of Jesus lead. That is why it is so necessary in an evangelistic meeting to push people to an issue of will. It is a terrible thing to awaken people up to a certain point and never give them the chance to act in the same atmosphere. If I preach a particularly searching discourse and never give the people a chance to act according to their inspired instincts at the time, their blood is on my head before God. If I make the issue clear and give them the opportunity to act, I clear my soul from their blood, whether they answer or not. The devil's counterfeit for this is wanting to see how many people we can get out to the penitent form. As preachers and teachers we have to bring people to the point of doing something.

(*b*) *The Inverting Impulse.* "No man having put his hand to the plough, and looking back, . . ."

Never postpone a moral decision. Second thoughts in moral matters are always deflections. Give as many second thoughts as you like to matters of prudence, but in the presence of God never think twice—*act*. Our Lord puts it very clearly in Matthew v. 23-24, when you are at the altar, i.e., in the presence of God, and your heart answers to the conviction of the Spirit of God, you know exactly what you must do: First go. There is no midway. If you say 'I don't mind going half-way, but I was not altogether in the wrong,' God's touch is gone instantly. The slightest revision of what I know God is telling me to do is the first element in the damnation of my character in that particular (see John iii. 19). Immediately I see what God wants me to do when I am in His presence, I must do it and care nothing for the consequences. "Lord, suffer me first to go and bury my father." The reply of Jesus sounds harsh, but remember the man's meaning was that he must stay with his father till he died. It was a point of view that put Jesus Christ right out of court. So with the rich young ruler, the wish to be all that Jesus wanted him to be awoke as soon as he came in contact with Him, but when it came to the first step of the will in acting it out, to become a mere conscious man, separated from all his wealth, dead fundamentally to the whole thing, then his countenance fell and he went away sorrowful. It is better never to have had the light than to refuse to obey it.

(*c*) *The Intrinsic Incapacity*. ". . . is fit for the kingdom of God."

'Not fit' does not mean, not good enough, it means out of the machine. We can never earn our place in the Kingdom of God by doing anything. Immediately we obey the instinct born in us of God's Spirit we are fitted into the Kingdom of God. Always act according to the wish that is born in you by the Spirit of God. Take the initiative to obey, never wobble spiritually. 'Wobble' means that we bring in other considerations that ought never to bemean the presence of God, because those

16

considerations mean that Jesus has not thought things out properly; He has forgotten I have a duty to my father and mother; that I have this thing the matter with my body; He has forgotten my circumstances. All these things are unconscious blasphemy against the Wisdom of God. We must always get to the point of acting on the want and the wish born in us when we are in the presence of Jesus Christ.

DIRECTION OF THE WILL

John vii. 17 (*R.V.*) (*cf. John* v. 19, 30.)

THE WILL TO DO.

"If any man willeth to do His will,"

In John vii. 17, our Lord is not so much laying down the principle that obedience is the gateway to knowledge, as specifically stating that the only way to know whether or not His teaching is of God is conditioned by obedience. The only way to *know* is to *will* to do His will.

(*a*) *Think.* The only way to progress in spiritual matters is to think voluntarily. A great amount of stuff we call thinking is not thinking, but merely reverie or meditation. Thinking is a voluntary effort, and in the initial stages it is never easy; voluntary effort must be made to keep the mind on some particular line. The teaching of some of the Higher Christian Life movements is apt to put thinking out of it altogether. According to that teaching we have to be semi-swooning invalids in the power of God, letting the Spirit of God take us as so much driftwood, and all our impulses and dreams are taken to be the will of God. When we become spiritual we have to exercise the power of thinking to a greater degree than ever before. We starve our mind as Christians by not thinking. If we are going to succeed in the natural world we must think voluntarily about things, and it is the same in the spiritual world. In order to think we must stop wool-gathering, check our impulses and set the mind on one line.

(b) Think *Habitually*. Habit is a mechanical process of which we have ceased to become conscious. The basis of habit is always physical. A habit forms a pathway in the material stuff of the brain, and as we persist in thinking along a certain line we hand over a tremendous amount to the machine and do things without thinking. Habit becomes second nature. "Habit a second nature! Habit is ten times nature!" (*Duke of Wellington*). For instance, when you begin to use a muscle in a particular way, it hurts badly, but if you keep on using that muscle judiciously it will get beyond hurting until you are able to use it with mechanical precision. The same thing is true in regard to thinking. It is a difficult matter to begin with. If thinking gives you a headache, it is a sign that you have brains. The brain is not ethereal or mystical, it is purely a machine. The thing that is not mechanical is the power of personality which we call thought. At first we find our brains do not work well, they go in jerks, we are bothered with associated ideas; but as we persist in thinking along a particular line our brain becomes the ally of our personality. Not only is our body capable of becoming our best friend, but the places where the body has become used to thinking become a strong assistance also. We infect the places we live in by our ruling habit. If we have made our body the ally of our personality, everything works together to aid our body wherever it is placed. People complain about their circumstances because they have not begun to make their body an ally.

(c) Think Habitually *to Do*. Our Lord says, in effect, that if any man will habitually think, he will come to know where His teaching comes from. The only way to prove spiritual truth is by experiment. Are we willing to set our mind determinedly to work out habitually what we think is God's will? We talk about justice and right and wrong, are we prepared to act according to what we think? Are we prepared to act according to the justice and the right which we believe to be the character of God? If we are, we shall have no difficulty in deciding whether or not the teaching of Jesus Christ comes from God.

The first moment of thinking alters our life. If for one moment we have discerned the truth, we can never be the same again; we may ignore it, or forget it, but it will not forget us. Truth once discerned goes down into the subconscious mind, but it will jump up in a most awkward way when we least expect it. In the matter of intercession, when we pray for another the Spirit of God works in the unconscious domain of that one's being about which we know nothing, and about which the one we pray for knows nothing, and after a while the conscious life of the one prayed for begins to show signs of softening and unrest, of enquiry and a desire to know something. It seems stupid to think that if we pray all that will happen, but remember to Whom we pray; we pray to a Being Who understands the unconscious depths of a man's personality, and He has told us to pray. The great Master of the human spirit said "Greater works than these shall he do; . . . and whatsoever ye shall ask in My name, that will I do." This is true also in preaching the word. We may see no result in our congregation, but if we have presented the truth and anyone has seen it for one second, he can never be the same again, a new element has come into his life. It is essential to remember this and not to estimate the success of preaching by immediate results.

Our Lord was always stern with disbelief, i.e., scepticism, because there is always a moral twist about scepticism.

Never place an agnostic in the same category as a sceptic. An agnostic is one who says, 'There is more than I know, but I have not found anyone who can tell me about it.' Jesus is never stern with that attitude; but He is stern with the man who objects to a certain way of getting at the truth because he does not like that way. If a man refuses to try the way Jesus Christ puts before him, he ceases from that second to be an honest doubter; he must try it and put Jesus Christ's teaching to the proof. A man cannot say he is an honest intellectual doubter if he refuses one way of getting at the truth; that is mental immorality.

THE WAY TO KNOW.

"he shall know of the teaching,"

If I find it hard to be a Christian it is a sign that I need the awakening of new birth. Only a spiritually ignorant person tries to be a Christian. Study the life of Jesus Christ and see what Christianity means, and you will find you cannot be a Christian by trying; you must be born into the life before you can live it. There are a great many people trying to be Christians; they pray and long and fast and consecrate, but it is nothing but imitation, it has no life in it. Immediately we have life imparted to us by the Holy Spirit, we realize that it is the very life that was in Jesus that is born into us; we are loosened from the old bondage and find that we can fulfil all the expectations of the life which has been imparted to us. It is a strenuous life of obedience to God, and God has given us bodies through which to work out the life, and circumstances to react against in order to prove its reality.

(a) *Intention.* Beware of praying about an intention-act. To pray about what we know we should do is to piously push the whole thing overboard and think no more about it. Every intention must be acted out *now*, not presently, otherwise it will be stamped out. When the intention of an honest soul is grasped by the Spirit of God he will know whether the teaching Jesus gives is of God or not. Am I going to *think*, and *think habitually*, and *act on what I think*, so that the will of God may be performed in me until I know Who Jesus is, and that His teaching is the teaching of God ? To know that the teaching of Jesus is of God means that it must be obeyed. It may be difficult to begin with, but the difficulty will become a joy.

(b) *Intention and Insight.* Intentions are born of listening to others. Whenever we obey an intention, insight into either good or bad is sure to follow. If our intention is in agreement with God and we act on it, we get insight into Who God is. The discernment of right and wrong intentions depends on how we think. There is a spasmodic type of life which comes from never really thinking about things, it is at the mercy of every stray intention. Someone makes an appeal for the Hindoo or the Chinese, and they say, ' Oh yes, I will go and preach the gospel there,' and they do it in intention. Then someone else says the best thing is to work in the slums, instantly their intention is to work there. Then another person says the best thing is to study in a Bible school, and they do that in intention. They are creatures of impulse, there is no real thinking along God's line, no acting on their intention. If you are sufficiently strong-minded you can generate any number of intentions in people and make them think anything you like ; if they are not in the habit of thinking for themselves you can always sway them. The power of an evangelist over men and women who do not think is a dangerous thing. That is why it is so perilous to tell people to yield. *Don't* yield! Keep as stiff a neck as ever you had, and yield to nothing and to no one, unless you know it is the Lord Jesus Christ to Whom you are yielding. Once you go on the yielding line, on the surrendering line and you do not know that it is the Lord Jesus Who is calling for the yielding, you will be caught up by supernatural powers that will wield you whether you like it or not. Woe be to you, if, when Jesus has asked us to yield to Him, you refuse; but be sure it is Jesus Christ to Whom you yield, and His demands are tremendous.

The insight that relates us to God arises from purity of heart, not from clearness of intellect. All the education under heaven will never give a man insight into Jesus Christ's teaching, only one thing will, and that is a pure heart, i.e., intentions that go along the right line. Education and scholarship may enable a man to put things well, but they will never give him insight. Insight only comes from a pure-heartedness in working out the will of God. That is why the subject of Divine guidance is so mysterious. "Be ye transformed by *the renewing of your mind*," says Paul, (that is what makes the thinker right), "that ye may prove what is that good, and acceptable, and perfect will of God." You cannot teach another what is the will of God. A knowledge of the will of God comes only by insight into God through acting on the right intention.

(c) *Intention and Insight into Instruction.* Studying our Lord's teaching will not profit us unless we intend to obey what we know is the immediate present duty. As we listen to certain interpretations of Jesus Christ's statements we do not feel warm to them, though we do not know what is wrong. Whenever the Spirit of God works in our conscious life it is like an intuition—I don't know how I know, but I know. The Holy Spirit witnesses only to His own nature, not to our reason. Jesus said

23

"My sheep hear My voice," not because it is argued to them, but because they have His Spirit. There are statements of Jesus which mean nothing to us just now because we have not been brought into the place where we need to understand them. When we are brought there, the Holy Spirit will bring back a particular word, and as we intend to obey He gives us the insight into it. The Spirit of God never allows us to face spiritual subjects by spiritual curiosity first. We cannot say, 'I am going to study the subject of Sanctification or of the Second Coming,' we shall make about as much headway as a steamer in a fog. Insight into the instruction of Jesus depends upon our intention to obey what we know to be the will of God. If we have some doctrine or some end of our own to serve, we shall always find difficulty.

The Weighing of Doctrine.

"whether it be of God, or whether I speak from Myself."

(a) *Discernment.* The reason the Incarnation and the Atonement are not credible to some people is that their disposition is unregenerated. A man may adopt the dogma of the Incarnation and the Atonement upon a basis of authority while his heart is unchanged, with the result that sooner or later the accumulated pride of unregenerate years will rise in revolt and secretly protest that it is incredible. That was the case with the men to whom Jesus is speaking here, and it is the case of hundreds who accept creeds but refuse to act on their belief; the consequence is they fling their creeds overboard and ignore the central test of Christianity, viz., Who is Jesus Christ to me?

The Atonement of our Lord never contradicts human reason, it contradicts the logic of human intellect that has never partaken of regeneration. The understanding of the Atonement depends not on Bible study, not on praying, but on spiritual growth. As we "grow up into Him in all things" we get moral understanding of the mystery of Redemption and understand why Jesus said "Blessed are the pure in heart, for they shall see God." The Spirit of God brings a man to the place where he begins to discern with his heart, not with his head.

Jesus says we shall know, i.e., discern, whether His teaching is of God or not when we do what we know to be His will. We discern according to our disposition. There are moments in life when the little thing matters more than anything else, times when a critical situation depends upon our attitude of mind to another person. If a man is hesitating between obeying and not obeying God, the tiniest thing contrary to obedience is quite sufficient to swing the pendulum right away from the discernment of Jesus Christ and of God. "If thou bring thy gift to the altar, and there rememberest that thy brother hath ought against thee . . . *first be reconciled* . . ." Distempers of mind make all the difference in the discernment of Jesus Christ's teaching. Have I a distempered view about any man or woman on earth? If I have, there is a great deal of Jesus Christ's teaching I do not want to listen to, then I shall never discern His teaching. Once let me obey God and I shall discern that I have no right to an attitude of mind to anyone other than His attitude. If I am determined to know the teaching of Jesus Christ at all costs, I must act on the intention that is stirred in me to do God's will, however humiliating it may be; and if I do, I shall discern.

(b) *Discernment of Inspiration.* Our Lord's teaching is God-breathed. What makes the difference between the attitude of a spiritual Christian to the teaching of Jesus and that of an unspiritual person? An unspiritual person takes the statements of Jesus to pieces as he would a man's statements, he "annulleth Jesus," dissolves Him by analysis (1 John iv. 3); a spiritual Christian confesses "that Jesus Christ is come in the flesh." The basis of membership in the early Church was discernment of Who Jesus is by the revelation of God (see Matthew xvi. 17–18). All through the test is, Do I know Who Jesus Christ is; do I know that His teaching is of God?

The mystery of the Bible is that its inspiration was direct from God (2 Peter i. 21). To believe our Lord's consciousness about Himself commits me to accept Him as God's last endless Word. That does not mean that God is not still speaking, but it does mean that God is saying nothing different from the Final Word, Jesus Christ; all God says expounds that Word.

(c) *Discernment of Inspiration of Christ's teaching.* Is Jesus Christ's teaching God-breathed to me? There is an intention that seeks God's blessings without obeying Jesus Christ's teaching. We are apt to say with sanctimonious piety, 'Yes, Jesus Christ's teaching is of God'; but *how do we measure up to it?* Do we intend to think about it and act on it? Beware of tampering with the springs of your life when it comes to the teaching of Jesus.

Purity of heart, not subtlety of intellect, is the place of understanding. The Spirit of God alone understands the things of God, let Him indwell, and slowly and surely the great revelation facts of the Atonement begin to be comprehended. The Mind of God as revealed in the Incarnation becomes slowly and surely the mind of the spiritual Christian.

FREEDOM OF THE WILL

Psalm xxvii. 4–6.

The subject of human free will is apt to be either understated or overstated. No man has the power to act an act of pure, unadulterated, free will. God is the only Being Who can act with absolute free will. The Bible reveals that man is free to choose, but it nowhere teaches that man is fundamentally free. The freedom man has is not that of power but of choice, consequently he is accountable for choosing the course he takes. For instance, we can choose whether or not we will accept the proposition of salvation which God puts before us; whether or not we will let God rule our lives; but we have not the power to do exactly what we like. This is easily demonstrated when we think of the number of vows that are made every New Year and so quickly broken.

Man is free to choose in so far as no human force can constrain him against his will. Pope is often misquoted; he did not say, "*Convince* a man against his will, he is of the same opinion still," but "*compel* a man against his will, he is of the same opinion still." God has so constituted man that it is not possible to convince him against his will; you can compel him and crush him, but you cannot convince him against his will. Only God could exercise constraint over a man which would compel him to do what in the moment of doing it is not his own will; but that God steadily refuses to do.

The reason man is not free is that within his personality there is a disposition which has been allowed to enslave his will, the disposition of sin. Man's destiny is determined by his disposition; he cannot alter his disposition, but he can choose to let God alter it. Jesus said, "Whosoever committeth sin is the servant of sin;" but He also said, "If the Son therefore shall make you free, ye shall be free indeed," i.e. free in essence. We are only free when the Son sets us free; but we are free to choose whether or not we will be made free. In the experience of regeneration a man takes the step of choosing to let God alter his disposition. When the Holy Spirit comes into a man, He brings His own generating will power and makes a man free in will. Will simply means the whole nature active, and when the Holy Spirit comes in and energizes a man's will, he is able to do what he never could do before, viz., he is able to do God's will. (Philippians ii. 13.)

THE UNIVERSE OF THE WILL.

"Thus not only our morality but our religion, so far as the latter is deliberate, depend on the effort which we can make." (James.)

Some propositions are alive to us and we want to work at them; other propositions are dead, they do not appeal to us at all. We have to be brought out of one universe of the will into another universe where propositions which were dead become alive. You can never tell when a proposition which up to a certain stage has been dead may suddenly become of living interest.

(a) *The Live Quest of the Will.* "One thing have I desired of the Lord, . . . that I may dwell in the house of the Lord all the days of my life,"

The depths of personality are hidden from our sight;

we do not know anything beyond the threshold of consciousness, God is the only One Who knows. When we try to go beyond our conscious life into the depths of our personality, we do not know where we are, our only refuge is the 139th Psalm—"Search me, O God, and know my heart." Whatever rouses your will is an indication of the bias of your personality. The Bible reveals that in a man's personality there is a bias that makes him choose not the proposition of godliness, but the proposition of ungodliness. This bias is not a matter of man's deliberate choice, it is in his personality when he is born. "Wherefore as by one man sin entered into the world . ." (Romans v. 12.) The proposition that appeals to a healthy once-born man is that of self-realization—'I want to develop myself.' If you bring before him the proposition that he should be saved and give up his right to himself to Jesus Christ, it will be a dead proposition, without meaning for him; but let conviction of sin, or disaster, or bereavement, or any of the great surprises of God touch him, and instantly the proposition takes on a totally new aspect and he will want to act on it. Jesus Christ always puts the emphasis on the effort of obedience, there must be a live quest of the will. 'If you want to know My doctrine, whether it is of God or of Myself, *do My will*,' says Jesus (see John vii. 17). The truth of God is only revealed to us by obedience.

(b) *The Lure of the Voluntary Quest.* "to behold the beauty of the Lord,"

When once the will is roused it always has a definite end in view, an end in the nature of unity. Always distinguish between will and impulse. An impulse has no end in view and must be curbed, not obeyed. Will is the whole effort of a man consciously awake with the definite end of unity in view, which means that body, soul and spirit are in absolute harmony. This end of

29

satisfaction offers a great fascination. The characteristic of a moral hell is satisfaction, no end in view, perfectly satisfied. Moral sickness is a perilous time, it is the condition to which sin brings us, and it accounts for the unutterable disappointments in life, there is no lure, no aim, no quest, no end in view. The characteristic of the spiritual life is the delight of discerning more and more clearly the end God has in view for us. Jesus did not say that eternal life was satisfaction, but something infinitely grander: "This is life eternal, that they might know Thee." The demand for satisfaction is God-given (cf. Matthew v. 6), but it must be satisfaction in the highest.

(c) *The Liberty to Question.* "and to inquire in His temple."

When once a man has been awakened from sin to salvation, the only propositions that are alive to his will are the propositions of God. There is an insatiable inquiry after God's commands, and to every command there is a desire to act in obedience. Recall your own experience and see how true that is. The things that used to be ends in view have not only ceased to be ends, they have ceased to have any interest for you at all; they have become tasteless. This is the way God enables us to be fundamentally dead to the things of the world while we live amongst them. Jesus Christ's outward life was densely immersed in the things of the world, yet He was inwardly disconnected; the one irresistible purpose of His life was to do the will of His Father.

If I am in right relationship to God there comes this delightful liberty of enquiring in His temple. It is not to be a Sabbath day spent in a temple, but the whole of the life, every domain of body, soul and spirit, is to be lived there. The dead set of the will is towards one end only, viz., to do the will of God. Jesus said, "My sheep hear My voice." When Jesus has not spoken there is an unutterable dullness all through, our spirit does not witness to what is being said. When once that fine balance of discernment is tampered with we give an opportunity to Satan; but if it is kept in perfect accord with God's word, He will guard. Jesus said that the Holy Spirit would bring His word to our remembrance (John xiv. 26). The Holy Spirit does not bring text after text until we are utterly confused; He simply brings back with the greatest of ease the words which we need in the particular circumstances we are in. Then comes in the use of the will, will I obey the word which has been brought back to our remembrance? The battle comes when we begin to debate instead of obeying. We have to obey and leave all consequences with God.

The Utmost Uses of the Will.

"Character exists only in so far as unity and continuity of conscious life exists, and manifests itself in systematic consistency of conduct." (Stout.)

Will is the very essence of personality, and in the Bible will is always associated with intelligence and knowledge and desire. The will of a saint is not to be spent in dissipation in spiritual luxuries, but in concentration upon God.

(a) *The Quietness of Strength.* "For in the time of trouble He shall hide me in His pavilion:"

God gives us the energy of an impregnable position, the heavenly places in Christ Jesus, and we have to make the effort to be strong from that position. We have not to work up to that position, but to work *from* it with the full energy of will. It is impossible to live according to our Lord's teaching without this secret of position. We do not get to the heavenly places by struggling, or aspiring, or consecration; God lifts us there, and if we will work from that position, He keeps us in His pavilion. No wonder the life of a saint appears such an unmitigated puzzle to rational human beings without the Spirit of God. It seems so ridiculous and so conceited to say that God Almighty is our Father and that He is looking after our affairs; but looked at from the position in which Jesus places us we find it is a marvellous revelation of truth.

(b) *The Quarters of Security*. "He shall set me up upon a rock."

In our spiritual life God does not provide pinnacles on which we stand like spiritual acrobats; He provides tablelands of easy and delightful security. Recall the conception you had of holiness before you stood by the grace of God where you do to-day, it was the conception of a breathless standing on a pinnacle for a second at a time, but never with the thought of being able to live there; but when the Holy Spirit brought you there, you found it was not a pinnacle, but a plateau, a broad way, where the provision of strength and peace comes all the time, a much easier place to live than lower down.

The security of the position into which God brings His saints is such that the life is maintained without ecstasy. There is no place for ecstasy and manifestations in a normal healthy spiritual life. The emotions that are beyond the control of the will are a sign that there is something not in the secure position, something undisciplined, untrained. When we are in the quarters of security we have to will our observation of the things of God, and of the way in which He works. There are things we are obliged to observe, such as fireworks; but God uses for the training of His children the things which we have to will to observe, viz., trees, and grass, and sparrows.

Never allow the idea of conscious straining effort when

you think of the exercise of the will spiritually. The straining effort comes in when we forget the great lines laid down by God. If you are a worker for God, Satan will try to wear you out to the last cell; but if you know God's grace you will be supernaturally recuperated physically. Recall how often you have been surprised, you thought you would have been exhausted after certain services, and instead, you became recreated whilst taking them. In this place of security there is no such thing as weariness without a corresponding recuperation if we maintain a right relationship with God.

(c) *The Quality of Supremacy*. "And now shall mine head be lifted up above mine enemies round about me:"

The supremacy over our old enemies is accounted for by the fact that God makes them our subjects. What things used to be your enemies? Stodginess of head, laziness of body or spirit, the whole vocabulary of 'I can'ts.' When you live in the right place these things are made your subjects; the things that used to hinder your life with God become subject to you by His power. The very things that used to upset you now minister to you in an extraordinary way by reason of the spiritual supremacy God gives you over them. The life of a saint reveals a quietness at the heart of things, there is something firm and dependable, because the Lord is the strength of the life.

HABIT

"In the conduct of life, habits count for more than maxims, because habit is a living maxim, become flesh and instinct. To reform one's maxims is nothing; it is but to change the title of the book. To learn new habits is everything for it is to reach the substance of life. Life is but a tissue of habits." (*Amiel.*)

MAN'S SOUL THE SCENE OF HABIT.

"Plasticity, then, in the wide sense of the word, means the possession of a structure weak enough to yield to influences, but strong enough not to yield all at once." (*James.*)

Beware of dividing man up into body, soul and spirit: man *is* body, soul and spirit. Soul has no entity, it depends entirely upon the body, and yet there is a subtle spiritual element in it. Soul is the rational expression of my personal spirit in my body, the way I reason and think and work. Habits are formed in the soul, not in the spirit, and they are formed in the soul by means of the body. Jesus Christ told His disciples that they must lose their soul, i.e., their way of reasoning and looking at things, and begin to estimate from an entirely different standpoint. For a while a born-again soul is inarticulate, it has no expression; the equilibrium has been upset by the incoming of a totally new spirit into the human spirit, and the reasoning faculties are disturbed. "In your patience possess ye your souls," says Jesus; that is, the new way of looking at things must be acquired with patience. On the basis of His Redemption Jesus Christ claims that He can put into my personal spirit His own heredity, Holy Spirit; then I have to form character on the basis of that new disposition. God will do everything I cannot do, but He will do nothing He has constructed me to do.

"Our virtues are habits as well as our vices." God does not give us our habits, but He holds us responsible, in proportion, for the habits we form. For instance, God does not hold a child born in the slums responsible in the same degree for its habits as He does a child born in a Christian home. The fact remains, however, that we form our own habits. God gives us a new disposition, but He gives us nothing in the shape of character. We have to work out what God works in, and the way we work it out is by the mechanical process of habit.

(a) *The Mental Phase.* Philippians iv. 8–9; 2 Corinthians x. 5.

By the mental phase is meant, thinking that can be stated in words. There is a great deal of thinking that cannot be expressed in words, such as that which is stirred by susceptibility to the beauties of Nature, or art or music; that is spirit not yet made rational in soul. We are responsible for our habits of thinking, and Paul in these passages is dealing with the phase of mental life in which a man can choose his thinking and is able to express it in words. The old idea that we cannot help evil thoughts has become so ingrained in our minds that most of us accept it as a fact. But if it is true, then Paul is talking nonsense when he tells us to choose our thinking, to think only on those things that are true, and honourable, and just, and pure.

"We may take as an example of mental habit that of

answering letters on the day on which they are received. Here what is habitual and automatic is not the process of writing the reply, but the writing of the reply on the same day on which the letter was received." (*Stout.*)

The point is that we make a mental decision to do a certain thing, and the habit of doing it grows until it becomes absolutely mechanical. Remember, then, we can and we must choose our thinking, and the whole discipline of our mental life is to form the habit of right thinking. It is not done by praying, it is done only by strenuous determination, and it is never easy to begin with.

(*b*) *The Moral Phase.* Romans vi. 11–19 (R.V.); 2 Peter i. 5–8 (R.V.).

The Spirit of God through the Apostles bases on the mechanism that is alike in everyone of us, the mechanism of habit. Paul says, "present your members as servants to righteousness;" Peter says, "adding on your part . . ." There is something we have to do. Man's soul is "weak enough to yield to influences, but strong enough not to yield all at once." The phrase 'the freedom of the will' is a catch phrase that has more of error than of truth in it. We are all so made that we can yield to an influence that is brought to bear upon us, and if we keep ourselves long enough under right influences, slowly and surely we shall find that we can form habits that will develop us along the line of those influences.

"The peculiarity of the moral habits, contradistinguishing them from the intellectual acquisitions, is the presence of two hostile powers, one to be gradually raised into the ascendant over the other. It is necessary, above all things, in such a situation, never to lose a battle. Every gain on the wrong side undoes the effect of many conquests on the right." (*Bain.*)

The idea is that of winding up a ball of wool. Let the ball drop, and infinitely more is undone than was wound in the same time. This is true of moral and spiritual habits. If once you allow the victory of a wrong thing in you, it is a long way back again to get readjusted. We talk on the moral and spiritual line as if God were punishing us, but He is not, it is because of the way God has constructed man's nature that "the way of transgressors is hard."

When once we begin the life with God on the moral line we must keep strictly to it. In the beginning the Holy Spirit will check us in doing a great many things that may be perfectly right for everyone else, but not right for us in the stage we are in. We have to narrow ourselves to one line, and keep ourselves narrow until our soul has gained the moral habit. The maimed life is always the characteristic to begin with (see Matthew v. 29–30), but our Lord's statements embrace the whole of the spiritual life from beginning to end, and in Matthew v. 48 (R.V.) He says, "*Ye therefore shall be perfect*, as your heavenly Father is perfect."

Never go contrary to your conscience, no matter how absurd it may be in the eyes of others. Conscience is to be our law in conduct, but Paul says it is not his own conscience, but the conscience of his weak brother that is his guide (1 Corinthians viii. 9–13).

The characteristic of a Christian is that he has the right not to insist on his rights. That will mean that I refuse to do certain things because they would cause my brother to stumble. To me the restrictions may be absurd and narrow-minded, I can do the things without any harm; but Paul's argument is that he reserves the right to suffer the loss of all things rather than put an occasion to fall in his brother's way. The Holy Ghost gives us the power to forgo our rights. It is the application of the Sermon on the Mount in practical life; if we are Jesus Christ's disciples we shall always do more than our duty, always do something equivalent to going ' the second mile.'

These are some of the moral habits we ought to form.

(c) The Mystical Phase. John xv. 4.

Our Lord did not say, 'Ask God that you may abide in Me;' He said "Abide in Me," it is something we have to do. Abiding in Jesus embraces physical, mental and moral phases as well as spiritual. How am I going to acquire the spiritual habit of union with Christ in God's sight? First of all by putting my body into the condition where I can think about it. We are so extraordinarily fussy that we won't give ourselves one minute before God to think, and unless we do we shall never form the habit of abiding. We must get alone in secret and think, screw our minds down and not allow them to wool-gather. Difficult? Of course it is difficult to begin with, but if we persevere we shall soon take in all the straying parts of our mental life, and in a crisis we shall be able to draw on the fact that we are one with Jesus in God's sight.

"One must first learn, unmoved, looking neither to the right nor left, to walk firmly on the strait and narrow path, before one can begin 'to make one's self over again.' He who every day makes a fresh resolve is like one who, arriving at the edge of the ditch he is to leap, forever stops and returns for a fresh run. Without *unbroken* advance there is no such thing as *accumulation* of the ethical forces possible, and to make this possible, and to exercise us and habituate us in it, is the sovereign blessing of regular work." (*Bahnsen.*)

In the mystical life the majority of us are hopeless wool-gatherers, we have never learned to brood on such subjects as 'abiding in Christ.' We have to form the habit of abiding until we come into the relationship with God where we rely upon Him almost unconsciously in every particular.

MECHANICAL SCIENTIFIC SIDE OF HABIT.

"Man is born with a tendency to do more things than he has ready-made arrangements for in his nerve-centres." (*James.*)

(*a*) *The Physical Side.* Job xiv. 19.

In physical nature there is something akin to habit. Flowing water hollows out for itself a channel which grows broader and deeper, and after having ceased to flow for a time, it will resume again the path traced before. It is never as easy to fold a piece of paper the first time as after, for after the first time it folds naturally. The process of habit runs all through physical nature, and our brain is physical. When once we understand the bodily machine with which we have to work out what God works in, we find that our body becomes the greatest ally of our spiritual life. The difference between a sentimental Christian and a sanctified saint is just here. The sanctified saint is one who has disciplined the body into perfect obedience to the dictates of the Spirit of God, consequently his body does with the greatest of ease whatever God wants him to do. The sentimental type of Christian is the sighing, tear-flowing, beginning-over-again Christian who always has to go to prayer meetings, always has to be stirred up, or to be soothed and put in bandages, because he has never formed the habit of obedience to the Spirit of God. Our spiritual life does not grow *in spite of* the body, but *because* of the body. "Of the earth, earthy," is man's glory, not his shame; and it is in the "earth, earthy" that the full regenerating work of Jesus Christ has its ultimate reach.

(b) *The Physiological Side.*   Mark ix. 21.

Every nervous affection makes a groove in the brain.
Dr. Carpenter, the great physiologist, suffered from
habitual neuralgia all the days of his life, the only time
he was free from it was when he was lecturing.   He said
himself it was simply because the nerves had got into the
habit.   What a medical man aims at in the case of nervous
affections is to forcibly cut short the attacks so as to give
the other physical forces possession of the field.   Nervous
trouble can be cured by sudden calamity, by something
that stops the whole nervous system and starts it again
in another way; and it can be cured suddenly by the power
of God.   In the case of the demoniac boy our Lord did
not deal with him on the medical line but on the supernatural line.   There was no gradual, 'take a little holiday,'
but a sudden and emphatic breaking off, simply because
our Lord recognised the way God has made the nervous
system.   No power on earth can touch a nervous trouble
if I have submitted to it for a long time, but God can touch
it if I will let Him.   I may pray for ever for it to be
altered but it never will be until I am willing to obey.
The arresting may be terrific, a tremendous break and
upset, but if I will let God have His way He will deal
with it.

(c) *The Psychical Side.*   Philippians ii. 12–13.

"Man is born with a tendency to do more things than
he has ready-made arrangements for in his nerve centres."

For instance, we are not born with a ready-made habit
of dressing ourselves, we have to form that habit.   Apply
that spiritually; when we are born again, God does not
give us a fully fledged series of holy habits, we have to
make those habits.   It is the application of the theological
statement that we have to transform innocence into holiness by a series of moral choices.   Ask yourself how much

time you have taken up asking God that you may not do the things you do. He will never answer, you have simply not to do them. Every time God speaks, there is something we must obey. We should do well to revise what we pray about. Some of the things we pray about are as absurd as if we prayed, 'O Lord, take me out of this room,' and then refused to go. We have to revise and see whether we intelligently understand what God has done for us; if He has given us the Holy Spirit, then we can do everything He asks us to do. If our body has been the slave of wrong habits physically, mentally and morally, we must get hold of a power big enough to re-make our habits and that power lies in the word 'Regeneration.' "If any man be in Christ, he is a new creature," that means this marvellous thing—that I may be loosened from every wrong habit I have formed if only I will obey the Spirit of God. Immediately I do obey, I find I can begin to form new habits in accordance with God's commands, and prove physically, mentally and morally that I am a new creation. That is why it is so necessary to receive the Holy Spirit, then when God gives a command it is sufficient to know He has told me to do it and I find I can do it. Frequently God has to say to us—'Say no more to Me on this matter; don't everlastingly cry to Me about this thing, do it yourself, keep your forces together and go forward.' God is for you, the Spirit of God is in you, and every place that the sole of your foot shall tread upon, shall be yours.

Beware of the luxury of spiritual emotions unless you are prepared to work them out. God does the unseen, but we have to do the seen.

DUST AND DIVINITY

Genesis ii. 7.

[N.B.—All divisions of the human personality
are arbitrary.]

Genesis ii. 7 reveals that man is made up of dust and
Divinity. This means that in practical psychology we
must always make allowance for the incalculable. You
cannot exhaust man's nature by examining his 'dust'
qualities, nor by describing him in terms of poetic sentiment, for after you have described as much as you can,
there is always an incalculable element to be taken into
account. There is more than we know, therefore we
cannot deal with ourselves as machines. One part of
ourselves must be dealt with as a machine, and the more
we deal with it as a machine the better; but to try and sum
up a man as a machine only is to miss out the bigger part;
or to say that man is altogether a spiritual being without
anything mechanical in him is to miss out the incalculable
element that cannot be summed up. These two things,
dust and Divinity, make up man. That he is made of the
dust is man's glory, not his shame; it has been the scene
of his shame, but it was designed to be his glory.

A certain type of mind gets impatient when one talks
about the incalculable element in man, and says it is
nonsense to talk of man being a spiritual personality, man
is nothing more than an animal. That outlook is pre-

valent to-day, it is called 'healthy-mindedness'; it is rather blatant ignorance. We all say what is obvious until we are plunged into the deeps; but when a man is profoundly moved he instantly finds himself beyond the reach of help or comfort from the obvious. The obvious becomes trivial, it is not what his heart wants. What he needs is something that can minister to the incalculable element. When once real thought begins to trouble the mind, the disturbance goes on throughout the whole personality until the right centre is gained for thought. In the spiritual domain when a man is convicted of sin, he realises that there are deeper depths in himself than he has ever known, and the things that can be clearly explained become utterly shallow, there is no guidance whatever in them. We begin by thinking we know all about ourselves, but when a man gets a dose of 'the plague of his own heart,' it upsets all his thinking. Immediately man begins to examine himself, he finds he is inscrutable; there are possibilities below the threshold of his life which no one knows but God.

THE EXPLORER OF THE WILL.

Philippians ii. 12–13.

Psalm cxxxix. is the classic in all literature concerning a man's personality. In this Psalm the tendency in man which makes him want to examine himself takes the form of prayer, 'O Lord, explore me.' The Psalmist implies: 'Thou art the God of the early mornings and late at nights, the God of the mountains and the fathomless deep; but, my God, my soul has farther horizons than the early mornings, deeper darkness than the nights of earth; higher heights than any mountain peaks, greater depths than any sea in nature; search *me* out, and see if there be any way of grief in me.' The Psalmist realised that God knew all

43

about the vast universe outside him, but there was something more mysterious to him than the universe outside, and that was the mystery of his own heart, and he asks the great Creator to come and search him. God does not search a man without he knows it, and it is a marvellous moment in a man's life when he is explored by the Spirit of God. The great mystic work of the Holy Spirit is in the dim regions of a man's personality where he cannot go. God Himself is the explorer of man's will, and this is how He searches us.

"It is God which worketh in you, both to will and to do of His good pleasure." 'Will' is not a faculty; 'will' is the whole man active, and the springs of will go deeper down than we can go. Paul says it is God who works in us to enable us to will, that is, the Holy Spirit, Who is the expression of God, will come into our spirit and energise our will so that we have power to actively will to do according to the standards of Jesus Christ. The Holy Spirit does not become our spirit; He invades our spirit and lifts our personality into a right relationship with God, and that means we can begin now to work out what God has worked in. The Holy Spirit enables us to fulfil all the commands of God, and we are without excuse for not fulfilling them. Absolute almighty ability is packed into our spirit, and to say 'can't,' if we have received the Holy Spirit, is unconscious blasphemy. We have not sufficiently realised the practical moral aspect of the Atonement in our lives. "If we walk in the light, as He is in the light"—then comes the amazing revelation, that "the blood of Jesus Christ His Son cleanseth us from all sin." Cleansing from all sin does not mean conscious deliverance from sin only, it means infinitely more than we are conscious of. The part we are conscious of is walking in the light; cleansing from all sin means something infinitely profounder, it means cleansing from all sin in the sight of God.   God never bases any of His work on our consciousness.

'Do you mean to tell me that God can search me to the inmost recesses of my dreams, my inmost motives, and find nothing to blame?   That God Almighty can bring the winnowing fan of His Spirit and search out my thoughts and imaginations, and find nothing to blame?' Who can stand before God and say, 'My hands are clean, my heart is pure?'   Who can climb that "hill of the Lord"?   No man under heaven, saving the man who has been readjusted at the Cross of Christ.   That man can stand before the scrutiny of God and know with a knowledge that passeth knowledge that the work of God's Son in him passes the scrutiny of God.   No soul ever gets there saving by the sovereign grace of God through the Atonement.

The Expression of the Conscience.

Acts xxiv. 16.

Conscience is that faculty in a man that attaches itself to the highest he knows and tells him what the highest he knows demands that he does.   Never be caught away with the phrase that conscience is the voice of God.   If it were, it would be the most contradictory voice human ears ever listened to.   Conscience is the eye of the soul and it looks out either towards God or towards what it regards as the highest, and the way conscience records is dependent entirely upon the light thrown on God (cf. Acts xxvi. 9 and xxiv. 16).

Take the case of a man who has had a great spiritual crisis and has entered into the experience of sanctification, his conscience is now looking towards God in the light that Jesus Christ throws upon God, what has he to do?

He has to walk in that light and begin to get his bodily machine into harmony with what his conscience records, that is, he has to walk now not in the light of his convictions, but in a purer sterner light, the light of the Lord. It is something he alone can do; God cannot do it for him. Supposing we say we believe God can give us the Holy Spirit and can energise our wills "to do of His good pleasure", instantly we see that, conscience records that we must obey. Any deflection in obedience to God is a sin. We have been used to doing things in this body in accordance with the old disposition—my right to myself, my self-interest; now we have to be regulated from a different standpoint. You did use the body as a servant to the wrong disposition, says Paul, see that you use it now as a servant to the right disposition (Romans vi. 19). It is never done suddenly. Salvation is sudden, but the working out of salvation in our life is never sudden. It is moment by moment, here a little and there a little. The Holy Spirit educates us down to the scruple.

Paul says he exercised himself to have "a conscience void of offence toward God and toward men". We have to endeavour to obey our conscience in our life of faith before God and in our life of fact before men. That does not mean we must not do things men will not like. Our conduct with men is measured by the way God has dealt with us, not by what men think of us. Our conscience will show us how God has dealt with us, "forgiving one another, even as God for Christ's sake hath forgiven you." That is the standard that is "void of offence toward God and toward men." Many of us are feeble Christians because we do not heed this standard. God works in the great incalculable element of our personality; we have to work out what He works in and bring it out into expression in our bodily life. It has not sufficiently entered into us that in our practical life we must do what

God says we must do, not try to do it, but *do it*, and the reason we can do it is that it is God Who works in us to will.

THE EXPECTATION OF THE HEART.

Psalm xxvii. 14; xlii. 5.

'Heart' is simply another term for 'personality.' The Bible never speaks of the heart as the seat of the affections. 'Heart' is best understood if we simply say 'me' (cf. Romans x. 10). When once expectation is killed out of the heart, we can scarcely walk, the feet become as lead, the very life and power goes, the nerves and everything begin to fall into decay. The true nature of a man's heart according to the Bible is that of expectation and hope. It is the heart that is strengthened by God (cf. Psalm lxxiii. 26), and Jesus Christ said that He came to "bind up the broken hearted." The marvel of the indwelling Spirit of God is that He can give heart to a despairing man. There is a difference between the human sympathy we give to a discouraged or broken-hearted man and what the Holy Spirit will do for him. We may sit down beside a broken-hearted man and pour out a flow of sympathy, and say how sorry we are for him, and tell him of other people with broken hearts; but all that only makes him more submissive to being broken-hearted. When our Lord sympathises with the heart broken by sin or sorrow, He binds it up and makes it a new heart, and the expectation of that heart ever after is from God.

The great discipline of our life spiritually is to bring other people into the realm of shadows. When God has brought other people into the realm of shadows, He can bring us into the relationship we need to be in towards Himself. The expectation of the heart must be based on this certainty: "In all the world there is none but thee, my God, there is none but thee." Until the human heart rests there, every other relationship in life is precarious and will end in heart-break. There is only one Being Who can satisfy the last aching abyss of the human heart, and that is the Lord Jesus Christ. The whole history of envy and cruelty in human relationships is summed up in the demand for infinite satisfaction from human hearts, we will never get it, and we are apt to become cruel, vindictive, bitter, and often criminal. When once the heart is right with God and the real centre of the life satisfied, we never expect or demand infinite satisfaction from a finite heart, we become absolutely kind to all other hearts and never become a snare. If our hearts are not rightly related to Jesus Christ, danger and disillusionment are on our track wherever we go, because other lives are not being led to God, they stick at us, they cannot get any further and they become enervated. But when once the heart is established in expectation on God, I defy other hearts to stick at you, they may try to, but all the time they are being led on to God Himself.

THE EXHORTATION OF THE MIND.

2 *Corinthians* x. 5. (R.V.).

Before a human spirit forms a mind it must express itself in words; immediately it expresses itself in words, it becomes a spirit of mind. In the natural man it is a spirit of mind "according to the flesh", but when the Holy Spirit energises a man's spirit, the words he expresses give him a mind "according to the spirit". When once the Spirit of God energises our spirit, we are responsible for forming the mind of Christ. God gives us the disposition of Jesus Christ, but He does not give us His mind, we have to form that, and we form it by the way we react on external things. "Let this mind be in you, which was also in Christ Jesus." Most of us baulk forming the mind of Christ; we do not object to being delivered from sin and hell, but we do object to giving up the energy of our minds to form the mind of Christ. The Holy Spirit represents the actual working of God in a man, and He enables us to form the mind of Christ if we will. We construct the mind of Christ in the same way as we construct the natural mind, viz., by the way our disposition reacts when we come in contact with external things.

The mind is closely affiliated with its physical machine, the brain, and we are responsible for getting that machine into right habits. 'Glean your thinking,' says Paul (see Philippians iv. 8). Never submit to the tyrannous idea that you cannot look after your mind; you can. If a man lets his garden alone it very soon ceases to be a garden; and if a saint lets his mind alone it will soon become a rubbish heap for Satan to make use of. Read the terrible things the New Testament says will grow in the mind of a saint if he does not look after it. We have to rouse ourselves up to think, to bring "every thought into captivity to the obedience of Christ." Never pray about evil thoughts, it will fix them in the mind. 'Quit'—that is the only thing to do with anything that is wrong; to ruthlessly grip it on the threshold of your mind and allow it no more way. If you have received the Holy Spirit, you will find that you have the power to bring "every thought into captivity to the obedience of Christ."

BEHAVIOUR

1 *Thessalonians* ii. 10.

THE FUNDAMENTAL RESOURCES OF PERSONALITY.

Behaviour means in its widest application every possible kind of reaction to the circumstances into which you may be brought.

There are resources of personality known only to God. Psalm cxxxix. is the prayer of a man asking God to explore him where he cannot go, and to garrison him. In 1 Thessalonians ii. 10, Paul is alluding to the working out of what God works in. The majority of us keep taking in and forget altogether that somehow we must work out what we take in: we cannot elude our destiny, which is practical. The profound nature of each one of us is created by God, but our perception of God depends entirely upon our own determined effort to understand what we come in contact with, and that perception is always coloured by the ruling disposition. If my ruling disposition is self-interest, I perceive that everything that happens to me is always for or against my self-interest; if, on the other hand, my ruling disposition is obedience to God, I perceive Him to be at work for my perfecting in everything that happens to me.

When my thought has been stirred by the Spirit of God and I understand what God wants me to be and experience the thrill that comes through the vision, I have to use my body to work out the vision. The first great psychological law to be grasped is that the brain and the body are pure mechanisms, there is nothing spiritual about them; they are the machines we use to express our personality. We are meant to use our brains to express our thought in words, and then to behave according to the way we have thought. A man's spirit only expresses itself as soul by means of words; the brain does not deal with pure thought. No thought is ours until it can be expressed in words. Immediately a thought is expressed in words, it returns to the brain as an idea upon which we can work. The type of life called the intellectual life is apt to deal only with these ideas, consequently there is a divorce from the practical life. The tyranny of intellect is that we see everything in the light of one principle, and when there is a gap, as there is in the moral development of man, the intellect has to ignore it and say these things are mere upsets. The Bible supplies the facts for the gap which the intellect will not accept. The intellect simply works on a process of logic along one line. Life is never a process of logic, life is the most illogical thing we know. The facts of life are illogical, they cannot be traced easily. Intellect is secondary, not primary. An intellectualist never pushes an issue of will.

We are not meant to spend our lives in the domain of intellectual thinking. A Christian's thinking ought never to be in reflection, but in activities. The philosopher says, 'I must isolate myself and think things out;' he is like a spider who spins his web and only catches flies. We come to right discernment in activities; thinking is meant to regulate the doing. Our destiny as spiritual men and women is the same as our destiny as natural men and women, viz., practical, from which destiny there is no escape.

Memory is a quality of personality; it does not exist in the brain but in the heart. The brain recalls more or less clearly what the heart remembers, and whether we can recall readily depends upon the state of our physical health. We take in through the words of others conceptions that are not ours as yet, we take them in through our ears and eyes and they disappear into the unconscious mind and become incorporated into our thinking. We say that the things we hear and read slip away from memory; they do not really, they pass into the unconscious mind. We may say at the time: 'I don't agree with that'; but if what we hear is of the nature of reality we will agree with it sooner or later. A truth may be of no use to us just now, but when the circumstances arise in which that truth is needed, the Holy Spirit will bring it back to our remembrance. This accounts for the curious way in which the statements of Jesus emerge; we say: 'I wonder where that word came from?' It came from the unconscious mind; the point is, are we going to obey it?

The matter of behaviour is ours, not God's. God does not make our character; character is formed by the reaction of our inner disposition to outer things through our nervous system. God does what we cannot do: He alters the mainspring and plants in us a totally new disposition; then begins our work, we must work out what God works in. The practising is ours, not God's. We have to bring the mechanism of body and brain into line by habit and make it a strong ally of the grace of God. We all know that it is never the grace of God that fails in a crisis; it is we who fail because we have not been practising. To refuse to form mental habits is a crime against the way we are made. It is no use praying, 'O Lord, give me mental habits.' God won't; He has made us so that we can make our own mental habits, if we will. When we are regenerated God does not give us another body, we have

52

the same body, and we have to get the bodily mechanism into working order according to His teaching. Think of the time we waste in talking to God and in longing to be what He has already made us instead of doing what He has told us to do!

"Be renewed in the spirit of your mind." The expression of the mind comes through the mechanism of the brain, and the marvellous emancipation that comes slowly and surely is that we have the power to do what God wants us to do. There is nothing that a man or woman energised by the Spirit of God cannot do. All the commandments of God are enablings. "If ye love Me, ye will keep My commandments," said Jesus; that is the practical simple test. Our Lord did not say, 'If a man *obeys* Me, he will keep My commandments'; but, "If ye *love* Me, ye will keep My commandments." In the early stages of Christian experience we are inclined to hunt with an overplus of zeal for commands of our Lord to obey; but as we mature in the life of God conscious obedience becomes so assimilated into our make-up that we begin to obey the commands of God unconsciously, until in the maturest stage of all we are simply children of God through whom God does His will for the most part unconsciously. Many of us are on the borders of consciousness—consciously serving, consciously devoted to God; all that is immature, it is not the life yet. The first stages of spiritual life are passed in conscientious carefulness; the mature life is lived in unconscious consecration. The term 'obey' would be better expressed by the word 'use.' For instance, a scientist, strictly speaking, 'uses' the laws of nature; that is, he more than obeys them, he causes them to fulfil their destiny in his work. That is exactly what happens in the saint's life, he 'uses' the commands of the Lord and they fulfil God's destiny in his life. The fundamental resources of personality will always stand true to God and to the way God has made us.

There are endless powers of reception in the deeper realms of personality where we cannot go, and it is these realms that God guards and garrisons. Personality is built to receive, it simply absorbs and absorbs; and education gives us the facility of expressing what we have received. We are designed with a great capacity for God, and the nature of personality is that it always wants more and more. Education is the drawing out of what is in for the purpose of expression, and we have to fit ourselves by acquired habits of conduct to express what we have received. What is the difference between an educated and an uneducated person? An educated person is one whose memory is so stored with abstract conceptions that whenever he is put into new circumstances, his memory instantly comes to his aid and he knows how to conduct himself. An uneducated person is nonplussed in new circumstances because he has nothing to come to his aid; whereas an educated person is able to extricate himself by means of examples with which his memory is stored and by the abstract conceptions he has formed of circumstances in which he has never been placed.

Apply it spiritually: Supposing you are asked to speak in the open air—'Oh, I can't!'; to take a Sunday School class—'Oh, I can't!'; to write an essay—'Oh, I can't!'; to expound a particular passage—'Oh, I can't!' What is the matter? we have not been educated on the right line. Some of us do not know what to do in certain circumstances spiritually because we have never stored our memory with the counsels of God, never watched the way God's servants conduct themselves. If we have been storing our minds with the word of God, we are never taken unawares in new circumstances because the Holy Spirit brings back these things to our remembrance and we know what we should do; but the Holy Spirit cannot bring back to our minds what we have never troubled to put there. "My people doth not consider," God says; they live on 'spooned meat' spiritually, go to church on Sunday and expect to live in the strength of it all the week without doing anything. We should be so in the habit of obeying the Holy Spirit as He interprets the word of God to us that wherever we are placed, we extricate ourselves in a holy and just and unblameable manner.

These things will always come to the rescue in the nick of time to the educated mind—the memory of how we have seen others act in the same circumstances, and the conceptions we form as we study God's Word. We do not become educated all at once, nor do we form habits all at once; it is done bit by bit, and we have to take ourselves strongly in hand. The one thing that keeps us back from forming habits is laziness. The lazy person in the natural world is always captious, and the lazy person spiritually is captious with God, 'I haven't had a decent chance.' Never let the limitation of natural ability come in. We must get to the place where we are not afraid to face our life before God, and then begin to work out deliberately what God has worked in. That is the way the habits which will show themselves in holy and just and unblameable behaviour are formed.

The Fit Reactions of Personality.

There is no reception without a reaction, and no impression without a corresponding expression. The great law regarding impressions and emotions is that if an emotion is not carried out on its own level, it will react on a lower level. The only test as to whether to allow an impression or emotion is to ask, What will this emotion

55

lead to if I let it have its way? Push it to its logical conclusion, and if the outcome is something God would condemn, grip it on the threshold of your mind as in a vice and allow it no more way. But if it is an emotion kindled by the Spirit of God, at the peril of your soul you refuse to act it out, because if you do not let that emotion have its right issue in your life, it will react on a lower level; whereas if you act an emotion out on its right level, you lift your whole life on to God's platform. Paul mentions gross immorality in close connection with sanctification because every devotional emotion not worked out on its own level will react on an immoral level secretly. This accounts for the fact that men and women whose private life is exceedingly wrong often show an amazing liking for devotional literature, for the writings of the saints, for the stirring of abstruse emotions. That is the way sentimentalists are made. Every emotion must express itself, and if it is not expressed on the right level, it will react on a lower level; and the higher the emotion, the more degraded the level on which it will react.

A saint is a bundle of specially qualified reactions. For every possible circumstance in life there is a line of behaviour marked out in advance for us; it is not stated in black and white, we have to be so familiar with God's Book that when we come to a crisis the Spirit of God brings back to our memory the things we had read but never understood, and we see what we should do. God is making characters, not mechanisms. We have to get our bodily mechanism into line with what God has worked in. The mighty work of God is done by His sovereign grace, then we have to work it out in our behaviour.

"Ye are witnesses, and God also, how holily and right-eously and unblameably we behaved ourselves toward you that believe." (1 Thessalonians ii. 10, R.V.) 'Unblame-able' does not mean faultless, it means a blameless disposition, undeserving of censure: that is, undeserving of censure in the sight of God Who sees everything. "Now unto Him that is able to guard you from stumbling, and to set you before the presence of His glory without blemish in exceeding joy." (Jude 24, R.V.)

ATTENTION

1 *Timothy* iv. 11–16.

Attention is never possible without conscious effort; interest frequently is, we can take up a book and our interest is riveted at once. Naturally we never attend to anything, we are like children, and children do not attend until they are taught to. We all have certain native interests in which we are absorbed; but attention is always an effort of will. We are held responsible by God for the culture of attention.

THE CAPACITY TO ATTEND.

"These things command and teach." (*v.* 11.)

Interest is natural; attention must be by effort, and the great secret of a Christian's life is the attention to realities. Reality is only possible where person comes in contact with person, all the rest is a shadow of reality. That is why Jesus said, '*I am the truth.*' When Saint Paul told Timothy to command and teach, he was building his counsel on this capacity to attend, which must be by effort. We are always more willing to get ideas from books and from other people, which is simply an indication that we are not willing to attend but prefer to have our natural interest awakened. We scoop other people's brains either in books or in conversation in order to avoid attending ourselves. One of our greatest needs is to have

58

a place where we deliberately attend; that is the real meaning of prayer. "Enter into thy closet, and when thou hast shut thy door, pray to thy Father which is in secret." Prayer that is not an effort of the will is un-recognised by God. "If ye abide in Me, and My words abide in you, ye shall ask what ye will and it shall be done unto you," said Jesus. That does not mean ask anything you like, but ask what you *will*. What are you actively willing? ask for that. We shall find that we *ask* very few things. The tendency in prayer to leave ourselves all abroad to the influence of a meeting or of a special season is not scriptural. Prayer is an effort of will, and Jesus Christ instructs us by using the word 'ask.' "Every one that asketh receiveth." These words are an amazing revelation of the simplicity with which God would have us pray. The other domains of prayer, the intercession of the Holy Spirit and the intercession of Christ, are nothing to do with us; the effort of our will is to do with us.

The Contemporary Attention.

"Let no man despise thy youth; but be thou an example of the believers," (*v.* 12.)

To-day men's attention is being screwed down along scientific lines; that is where the effort is being made. Think of the sweat and labour that a scientific student will expend in order to attain his end; where do we find men and women concentrating with the same intensity on spiritual realities? The majority of us are totally ignorant of the one abiding reality that demands our attention, viz., our relationship to God, which should exhibit itself in a life in accordance with that relationship. The essence of sin is the refusal to recognise that we are accountable to God at all. The relationship to God must be recog-nised and lived up to from the crown of the head to the soles of the feet; nothing is unimportant in this relationship.

"Let no man despise thy youth," Paul said to Timothy. Youth is a thing to be despised, a man up to thirty ought to be shut up in a bandbox and not allowed to speak. Paul is not saying, 'Stand up for your rights;' not, 'Let no man despise thy youth because you are as good as anybody else, but by being an example in word, in conversation, in charity, in spirit, in faith and in purity to all who believe the realities which you believe; don't be caught up by contemporary attentions.' It is so easy to attend to the thing every one else is attending to, but it is difficult to attend to what no one is attending to. Paul did not say, 'Pay attention to the Greek philosopher, to the history of your people,' to the thousand and one things that were contemporary in his day; he said, 'Screw your attention with all your effort on the one reality, your relationship to God, and be an example on that all through.'

THE COMMISERATING ATTENTION.

"Give attendance to reading," (v. 13.)

How many of us spend our time expecting that we will be something we are not. 'Oh the time is coming when I am going to be so and so.' It never will come; the time is always *now*. The amazing thing about the salvation of our Lord is that He brings us into contact with the reality that is, until we are just like children, continually seeing the wonder and beauty of things around us. The characteristic of young men and women of to-day is an affected tiredness of everything, nothing interests them. The salvation of Jesus is not a Divine anticipation, it is an absolute fact. People talk about the magnificent ideals that are yet to be; but the marvel of being born from above is that the reality is infinitely more wonderful than all we have imagined. Our Lord taught us to look at such things as grass and trees and birds; grass is not ideal, it is real; flowers are not ideal, they are real; sunrises and sunsets are not ideal, they are real. These things are all round about us, almost pressing themselves into our eyes and ears, and yet we never look at them. Jesus Christ drew all His illustrations from His Father's handiwork, from sparrows and flowers, things that none of us dream of noticing; we take our illustrations from things that compel attention. When we are born from above the Spirit of God does not give us new ideals, we begin to see how ideal the real is; and as we pay attention to the things near at hand, we find them to be the gate of heaven to our souls. The reality of the salvation of Jesus Christ is that He makes us pay attention to realities, not appearances.

The Soul's Awakening.

"Neglect not the gift that is in thee," (v. 14.)

There is a difference between such books as Trine's *"In Tune with the Infinite"* and the reality of life. It is possible to go dreaming through life till we are struck, not by an ideal, but by a sudden reality, and all we have ever pictured of what a man or woman should be pales before the reality we see. That is what happened when men saw Jesus Christ in the days of His flesh. The Spirit of God saves us from the absurd futility of useless tears when the near objects have become far by making us open our eyes to what is near. We weep around the graves of people and things because we have never realised that we have to pay attention to the reality that is at hand. Take a lad who has become impatient with his home, he is sick of it, he cannot stand his parents, his sisters are prosaic, and he leaves—the best thing for him. Let him come in contact with other people's fathers and mothers and sisters—Oh, yes, he much prefers them; but he will soon come to realise that the ones he has left are infinitely better. Naturally we much prefer the friends we make to our God-made relations, because we can be noble with our friends, we have no past history with them.

This principle works all through. We long for something that is not and shut our eyes to the thing that is. When the Lord Jesus awakens us to reality by new birth and brings us in contact with Himself, He does not give us new fathers and mothers and new friends; He gives us new sight, that is, we focus our eyes on the things that are near and they become wonderfully distant. "Put thy distance on the near." This craving to go somewhere else, to see the things that are distant, arises from a refusal to attend to what is near.

Have I ever realised that the most wonderful thing in the world is the thing that is nearest to me, viz., my body? Who made it? Almighty God. Do I pay the remotest attention to my body as being the temple of the Holy Ghost? Remember our Lord lived in a body like ours. The next reality that I come in contact with by my body is other people's bodies. All our relationships in life, all the joys and all the miseries, all the hells and all the heavens, are based on bodies; and the reality of Jesus Christ's salvation brings us down to the Mother Earth we live on, and makes us see by the regenerating power of God's grace how amazingly precious are the ordinary things that are always with us. Master that, and you have mastered everything. We imagine that our bodies are a hindrance to our development, whereas it is only through our bodies that we develop. We cannot express a character without a body.

This is also true of Nature. We do not get at God through Nature, as the poets say, we get at Nature through God when once we are rightly related to Him, and Nature becomes a sacrament of His Presence. Such books as Trine's start at the wrong end, they try to bring us from the ideal to the real; it is by coming in contact with the real that we find the ideal.

"Neglect not the gift that is in thee." We have to be careful not to neglect the spiritual reality planted in us by God. The first thing that contact with reality does is to enable us to diagnose our moods. It is a great moment when we realize that we have the power to trample on certain moods. Moods never go by praying, moods go by kicking. A mood nearly always has its seat in the physical condition, not in the moral, and it is a continual effort to refuse to listen to those moods which arise from a physical condition; we must not submit to them for a second. It is a great thing to have something to neglect in your life; a great thing for your moral character to have something to snub. "The expulsive power of a new affection"—that is what Christianity supplies. The Spirit of God on the basis of Redemption gives us something else to think about. Are we going to think about it?

By heeding the reality of God's grace within us we are never bothered again by the fact that we do not understand ourselves, or that other people do not understand us. If anyone understood me, he would be my god. The only Being Who understands me is the Being Who made me and Who redeems me, and He will never expound me to myself; He will only bring me to the place of reality, viz., into contact with Himself, and the heart is at leisure from itself for ever afterwards.

The first things a Christian is emancipated from is the tyranny of moods and the tyranny of feeling that he is not understood. These things are the most fruitful sources of misery. Half the misery in the world comes because one person demands of another a complete understanding, which is absolutely impossible. The only

Being Who understands us is the Being Who made us. It is a tremendous emancipation to get rid of every kind of self-consideration and learn to heed only one thing, the relationship between God and ourselves. "In all the world there is none but thee, my God, there is none but thee." Once we get there, other people become shadows, beautiful shadows, but shadows under God's control.

THE SCRIPTURAL ATTITUDE.

"Meditate upon these things;" (v. 15.)

Meditation means getting to the middle of a thing, pinning yourself down to a certain thing and concentratedly brooding upon it. The majority of us attend only to the 'muddle' of things, consequently we get spiritual indigestion, the counterpart of physical indigestion, a desperately gloomy state of affairs. We cannot see anything rightly, and all we do see is stars. "Faith is . . . the evidence of things not seen." Suppose Jesus suddenly lifted the veil from our eyes and let us see angels ministering to us, His Own Presence with us, the Holy Ghost in us, and the Father around us, how amazed we should be! We have lived in the 'muddle' of things instead of in the middle of things. Faith gets us into the middle, which is God and God's purpose. Elisha prayed for his servant, "Lord, I pray Thee, open his eyes, that he may see", and when his eyes were opened he saw the hosts of God and nothing else.

We have to learn to pay attention to reality; one soul attending to reality is an emancipation to hundreds more. We are impertinently inquisitive about everything saving that one thing. Through inattention to our own true capacity we live as in a dream, when all around us and in us are the eternal realities. 'Attend to these duties, let them absorb you, so that all men may note your progress.'

We are apt to be busy about everything but that which concerns our spiritual progress, and at the end of a profitless day we snatch up a Bible or Daily Light and read a few verses, and it does us good for precisely three-quarters of a second. We have to take time to be diligent. Meditation is not being like a pebble in a brook, allowing the waters of thought to flow over us; that is reverie. Meditation is the most intense spiritual act, it brings every part of body and mind into harness. To be spiritual by effort is a sure sign of a false relationship to God; to be obedient by effort in the initial stages is a sure sign that we are determined to obey God at all costs. Take time. Remember we have all the time there is. The majority of us waste time and want to encroach on eternity. 'Oh well, I will think about these things when I have time.' The only time you will have is the day after you are dead, and that will be eternity. An hour, or half an hour, of daily attention to and meditation on our own spiritual life is the secret of progress.

THE SACRED ATTENTION.

"Take heed unto thyself." (v. 16.)

If we have been living in unrealities, we shall find ourselves faced with a great impatience when we do endeavour to face reality, and we are apt to behave like caged wild beasts. We have to take a grip of ourselves when we come to the true centre of things, and it means discipline *and discipline*, until we face nothing but realities. We have to exert a tremendous effort, and God is pleased to see us exert it. If you try and settle down before God in prayer when you have been dwelling in unrealities, you will recognise instantly the condition of things. As soon as you get down to pray you remember a letter you ought to write, or something else that needs to be done, a thousand and one little impertinences come in and claim your attention. When we suspend our own activities and get down at the foot of the Cross and meditate there, God brings His thoughts to us by the Holy Spirit and interprets them to us. The only mind that understands the things of God is the child mind (see Matthew xi. 25); our Lord continually mentioned this simplicity (see Matthew xviii. 3). It is the simplicity of God, not of an imbecile, a fundamental simplicity of relationship. God has not the remotest opportunity of coming to some of us, our minds are packed full with our own thoughts and conceptions; until suddenly He comes in like the wind and blows all our thoughts right away, and thoughts come sauntering in from the Word of God. We can never get those thoughts for ourselves. They are the free gift of God for anyone and everyone who is learning to pay attention to Him.

NATURAL GROWTH IN SUPERNATURAL GRACE

1 *Peter* ii. 7–12.

Our Lord's maxims
{ "*Consider the lilies of the field, how they grow*"
"*Behold the fowls of the air.*"
"*Become as little children.*" }

Our Lord did not point out wonderful sights to His disciples all the time; He pointed out things that were apparently insignificant—lilies, and grass, and sparrows. God does not deal with the things that interest us naturally and compel our attention; He deals with things which we have to will to observe. The illustrations Jesus Christ used were all taken from His Father's handiwork because they express exactly how the life of God will develop in us. We draw our illustrations from the works of men, consequently we get into a hustling condition and forget our Lord's maxims.

"Consider the lilies of the field, how they grow"—in the dark! We are apt to consider a lily when it is in the sunshine only, but for the greater part of the year it is buried in the ground; and we imagine that we are to be always above ground, shedding perfume and looking beautiful; or continually being cut and put into God's show-room to be admired, forgetting altogether that we cannot be as lilies unless we have spent time in the dark, totally ignored.   As a disciple, Jesus says, consider your hidden life with God.   When we breathe fresh air we are not consciously exhilaratingly different all the time; but if we continue to take in fresh air, it makes a profound difference.   This is true of our life in Christ.   If we receive the Holy Spirit and obey Him, He makes a profound difference, and it will be manifested one day as a great surprise.   It is not done in a minute as far as our consciousness is concerned, but when we come to a crisis we find to our astonishment that we are not upset or perplexed, as we might have expected, but we realise that our whole outlook has been altered.   The Spirit of God awaits His own time to bring the crisis, we are apt to say, 'I want the crisis now.'   We shall never see God's point of view as long as we bring our own ideas to Him and dictate to God what we expect Him to do.   We must become as little children, be essentially simple, keep our minds brooding on what God tells us to brood on, and let God do as He likes.   The difficulties come because we will not be simple enough to take God at His word.

Our natural reactions are not wrong, although they may be used to express the wrong disposition.   God never contradicts our natural reactions; He wants them to be made spiritual.   When we are saved God does not alter the construction of our bodily life, but He does expect us to manifest in our bodily life the alteration He has made. We express ourselves naturally through our bodies, and we express the supernatural life of God in the same way, but it can only be done by the sacrifice of the natural. How many of us are spiritual in eating and drinking and sleeping?   Those acts were spiritual in our Lord; His relationship to the Father was such that all His natural life was obedient to Him, and when He saw that His Father's will was for Him not to obey a natural reaction, He instantly obeyed His Father (see Matthew iv. 1–4).

If our Lord had been fanatical He would have said—'I have been so long without food, I will never eat again.' That would have been to obey a principle instead of God. When God is educating us along the line of turning the natural into the spiritual, we are apt to become fanatical. Because by God's grace things have been done which are miraculous, we become devoted to the miracle and forget God, then when difficulties come we say it is the antagonism of the devil. The fact is we are grossly ignorant of the way God has made us. All that we need is a little of what we understand by pluck in the natural world put into the spiritual. Don't let your body get on top and say there is nothing after all in what God said. Stand up to the difficulty, and all that you ever believed about the transforming grace of God will be proved in your bodily life.

CURIOSITY.

v. 7.

Curiosity is the desire to come to a full knowledge and understanding of a thing; it is a natural reaction. Imagine a child without curiosity! A child cannot sit and listen to a lecture, but let him see something bright and instantly he is curious and wants to get hold of it, whether it is the moon or a ball. The reaction is based not so much on the desire to have it for himself as on the desire to know more about it. As men and women we are curious about intellectual or philosophic or scientific things, and when a particular quality is presented our curiosity is aroused—'I want to know more about this matter, can anyone explain it to me satisfactorily?' It is the natural reaction of the way we are made, and to ignore it is fanatical. The instinct of curiosity can be used in the wrong way (see Genesis iii. 6), but that does not mean that the reaction itself is wrong, it depends upon the motive. A point that is frequently missed in dealing with the questions of a child is that he asks them from a disinterested motive; a teacher can always appeal to the disinterested curiosity of a child. A child's questions are at the very heart of things, questions that scarcely occur to a philosopher.

In natural life we grow by means of curiosity, and spiritually we grow by the same power. The Spirit of God uses the natural reaction of curiosity to enable us to know more about the One Who is precious. The instinct is not denied, but lifted on to a different platform and turned towards knowing Jesus Christ. As saints our curiosity must not be all abroad; we become insatiably curious about Jesus Christ; He is the One Who rivets our attention. Think of the avidity with which you devour anything that has to do with expounding the Lord Jesus Christ,—"unto you therefore which believe He is precious."

IMITATION.

v. 9.

Imitation is one of the first reactions of a child, it is not sinful. We come to a right knowledge of ourselves by imitating others. The instinct that makes us afraid of being odd is not a cowardly instinct, it is the only power of self-preservation we have. If you live much by yourself you become an oddity, you never see the quirks in yourself. Some people won't live with others spiritually, they live in holes and corners by themselves. The New Testament warns of those who "separate themselves" (Jude 19). By the grace of God we are taken out of the fashion we were in and we become more or less speckled birds. Immediately you introduce a standard of imitation which the set to which you belong does not recognise, you will experience what Peter says, "they think it strange

that ye run not with them to the same excess of riot"
(1 Peter iv. 4).

The Spirit of God lifts the natural reaction of imitation
into another domain and by God's grace we begin to
imitate Our Lord and shew forth His praises. It is the
natural instinct of a child to imitate his mother, and when
we are born again the Holy Spirit lifts this instinct into
the spiritual domain and it becomes the most supernaturally natural thing for us to imitate our Lord. We
grow in grace naturally, not artificially. Mimicking is
the counterfeit of imitation and produces the 'pi' person,
one who tries his level best to be what he is not. When
you are good you never try to be. It is natural to be like
the one we live with most; then if we spend most of our
time with Jesus Christ, we shall begin to be like Him,
by the way we are built naturally and by the Spirit God
puts in.

EMULATION.

v. 9.

Emulation is the instinct to imitate what you see
another doing, in order not to appear inferior. A boy
who accepts the place of inferiority is either lazy or is
becoming heartbroken; he has no right to sink down and
submit to being inferior, he is not built that way naturally.
A child always admires anyone with skill, and the teacher
who says, 'Do this and that,' has no influence over a child
compared with the one who says, 'Come and do this with
me.' When a child has seen his teacher do a thing and
is asked to do it, instantly the instinct of emulation is at
work.

Our Lord builds His deepest teaching on the instinct
of emulation. When His Spirit comes in He makes me
desire not to be inferior to Him Who called me. Our
example is not a good man, not even a good Christian

man, but God Himself. By the grace of God I have to emulate my Father in heaven. "Be ye therefore perfect, even as your Father which is in heaven is perfect" (Matthew v. 48). The most natural instinct of the supernatural life of God within me is to be worthy of my Father. To say that the doctrine of sanctification is unnatural is not true, it is based on the way God has made us. When we are born again we become natural for the first time; as long as we are in sin we are abnormal, because sin is not normal. When we are restored by the grace of God it becomes the most natural thing to be holy, we are not forcing ourselves to be unnatural. When we are rightly related to God all our natural instincts help us to obey Him and become the greatest ally of the Holy Spirit. We disobey whenever we become independent. Independence is not strength but unrealised weakness, and is the very essence of sin. There was no independence in our Lord, the great characteristic of His life was submission to His Father.

Emulation and imitation both centre around whatever is our ideal. When once we see Jesus, it is good-bye to all ideals; we cannot have them back again, nor do we want them back again if we are true to Him. We have to keep the one Lodestar, the Lord Jesus Christ, in front and be absorbingly taken up with Him ; consequently we have to put ourselves through discipline and fast from every other type of emulation.

AMBITION.

v. 11.

Ambition is a mixture of pugnacity and pride, a reaction of unwillingness to be beaten by any difficulty. It is a natural reaction. Think of a boy without the instinct to fight! The reaction that makes one boy punch another is not bad, although the disposition behind it may be.

The natural reaction of ambition in a man or woman saved by God's grace is that they will not be beaten by anything the world, the flesh or the devil can put in the way of their fulfilling God's idea for them. By the grace of God we get to the place where we do not punch other people, but punch the devil clean out of the arena. "Resist the devil." How can we resist the devil unless we are ambitious not to be beaten by him? When we become spiritual the reaction of pugnacity is lifted on to another plane and we say to our body, 'It can be done and it shall be done' (cf. 1 Corinthians ix. 27). Most of us are devoid of spiritual pluck. Many who are naturally plucky lose all their pluck when they get a smattering of grace and become sentimental and pathetic, every tiny ache which they would have ignored altogether before they were saved, is of the devil! God does not tell us to leave the natural life entirely alone; the natural life has to be turned into the spiritual, and it is because we do not realise this that we become whining people spiritually where we would have scorned to whine naturally.

When we are born into the kingdom of God we realise that we are not fighting against flesh and blood, but against spiritual enemies, "against spiritual wickedness in high places." The Book of The Revelation is based on the reaction to overcome. "To him that overcometh . . ." You cannot overcome if there is nothing to overcome. In natural education everything is built up on difficulty, there is always something to overcome. And this is true in the spiritual world. If the world, the flesh and the devil have knocked you out once, get up and face them again, and again, until you have done with them. That is how character is made in the spiritual domain as well as in the natural. Our prayers for God's help are often nothing but incarnate laziness, and God has to say, "Speak no more unto Me of this matter.   Get thee up . . ."

The pugnacious element is a natural reaction, and as Christian teachers we have to recognise it.   Ambition in the spiritual domain is the reaction which refuses to bow its neck to any yoke but the yoke of the Lord Jesus Christ.   Nothing awakens scorn amongst men more than a quitter, one who funks in a game.   Weakness or imbecility do not awaken contempt as much as one sign of the white feather, a refusal to face the music, the tiniest sign of the lack of pugnacity.   The law of antagonism runs all through life, physical, moral, mental and spiritual. I am only healthy according to the fighting corpuscles in my blood, when the fighting millions inside get low, I become diseased and after a while I shall be snuffed out. Morally it is the same, we are not born moral, we are born innocent and ignorant; morality is the outcome of fight. Immediately I am lazy in moral matters, I become immoral.   Spiritually it is the same.   "In the world ye shall have tribulation:"—everything that is not spiritual makes for our undoing—"but be of good cheer; I have overcome the world."   Why did not our Lord say that He would help us to overcome?   Because we have to imitate Him through the power He has put in us.   Think of sitting in a corner before the Almighty and saying, 'But my difficulties are so enormous.'   Thank God they are!   The bigger the difficulty, the more amazing is your profit to Jesus Christ as you draw on His supernatural grace.

OWNERSHIP.

vv. 11–12.

The instinct of ownership is seen from the first of life to the last.   As soon as an infant tongue can say anything, it will say 'me' and 'mine'.   'Is this mine?'   'Yes';—

then expect to see it smashed. The child wishes you to understand that he can do what he likes with his own. It is only the discipline of life that teaches us to keep things. The instinct of ownership is a right one, though the disposition expressed through it may be wrong. In a saint the idea of ownership is that we have the power to glorify God by good works (see Matthew v. 16). What we own is the honour of Jesus Christ. Have I ever realised that His honour is at stake in my bodily life? "What? know ye not that your body is the temple of the Holy Ghost which is in you. . . . ?" Do I own my body for that one purpose? do I own my brain to think God's thoughts after Him? We have to be intensely and personally God's.

The Spirit of God brings us into the realisation of our ownership, and the instinct of ownership becomes a tremendous wealth in the life. "All things are your's," and Paul prays that the eyes of our understanding may be enlightened that we may know what is ours in Christ Jesus.

No personality, from a tiny child to Almighty God, is without this sense of ownership. How wonderfully sprightly a dog looks when he is owned! How weary and hang-dog we become when we are convicted of sin; but when we experience God's salvation, we straighten up immediately, everything is altered, we can fling our heads back and look the world in the face because the Lord Jesus Christ is ours and we are His. A dominant ownership, such as the ownership of the Lord means that we own everything He owns. "The meek shall inherit the earth."

THE WAY OF A SOUL

Ephesians v. 14–18.

THE WAY OF THE AWAKENING OF THE SOUL.

"Awake thou that sleepest, and arise from the dead." (v. 14–15.)

What is Possible in the Way of Habits. A good many of us are in the condition that St. Augustine described himself to be in, the condition of a half-awakened man who does not wish to be awakened—"a little more sleep." God smote St. Augustine with the words, "not in chambering and wantonness." When the Spirit of God brings a word of God to us, are we going to wake up and lay hold of it, or remain in the condition St. Augustine was in—"a little more worldliness; a little less intensity"? If God tells us to awake, we must get into the habit of awakening. We have to wake up physically before we can wake up spiritually. When God tells us to do a thing He empowers us to do it, only we must do the doing. Think of the number of times we say, 'Oh, I can't.' For the good of your own soul, say 'I won't.' To say, 'I can't' enervates the whole life. If we really cannot, God has misled us. Jesus said "All power is given unto Me"; if He tells us to do something and we cannot, this is simply not true.

We talk about attacks of the devil—'I cannot concentrate my mind, the devil hinders me.' The reason we cannot concentrate is that we are culpably ignorant about ourselves. The devil does not need to bother about us as long as we remain ignorant of the way God has made us and refuse to discipline ourselves; inattention and our own slovenliness will soon run away with every power we have. Watch the care students take in other domains of life, and then think of our own laziness and the way we continually fall back and say, 'It can't be done.' All we need is grit and gumption and reliance on the Holy Spirit. We must bring the same determined energy to the revelations in God's Book as we bring to earthly professions. Most of us leave the sweat of brain outside when we come to deal with the Bible.

Anything and everything is possible in the way of habits. Habits form a pathway in the material stuff of the brain. We cannot form a habit without thinking about it; but when once the pathway in the brain is formed we can do a thing easily without thinking about it. For instance, we were not born with the ready-made habit of dressing ourselves, we had to form that habit. If we persist in using our bodies in a certain way, alterations will take place in the make-up of the brain. Spiritually we have to learn to form habits on the basis of the grace of God. What happens at new birth is that the incoming of a totally new life breaks all the old habits, they are completely dislodged by the "expulsive power of a new affection." Most of us do not realise this and we continue to obey habits when there is no need to. The incoming of the Spirit of God from without forms a disassociation physically, and new habits can be formed. Never dispute for a second when God speaks; if you debate, you give an opportunity to the old habits to re-assert themselves. Launch yourself with as strong an initiative as possible on the line of obedience; it is difficult at first, but immediately you start to obey, you find you can do it. The danger is to say 'I can't,' or, 'I will do it presently.' When in your soul's vision you see clearly what God wants, let me advise you to do something physical immediately. If you accompany a moral or spiritual decision with a physical effort, you give the necessary initiative to form the new habit. A physical exertion is imperative in spiritual transactions, otherwise it is in danger of passing into thin air. When God tells you to do a thing, never wait for a fitting opportunity, *do it now.* You may dream about doing it to further orders, the only thing to do is to launch out at once and make things inevitable, make it impossible to go back on the decision.

Beware of divorcing the physical and the spiritual. Habits are physical, and every command of God has a physical basis. "He that hath ears to hear, let him hear." You cannot hear with your heart if you do not listen with your physical ears. Does God find me quick in the uptake to discern what He says? Am I awake enough to hear? God always locates His spiritual revelations in a physical body. The great God became Incarnate in flesh and blood; the great thoughts of God became crystallized in words. When the Spirit of God touches us, we are responsible for forming the mind of Christ. God does the wonderful indwelling part, but we have to do the expressing (see Philippians ii. 12–13), and when once we understand how God has made us, it becomes not at all difficult to do it. The Spirit of God knocks and says, 'Wake up, form this habit,' and if you try, you find you can because you find you have a wealth of power within. It is only when we are willing to be identified with the death of Jesus that the full power of His life is able to work, and we find a new page of consciousness open in our lives. There are new forces in us and we are able now to do what we never could before; we are free from the old bondage and limitations. The gateway into this life is through the death of Jesus Christ.

Be a saint physically.

"understanding what the will of the Lord is." (v. 16–17.)

What is possible in the Way of Intelligence. Have we begun to form the habit of thinking? Thinking is the habit of expressing what moves our spirit. In order to think we must concentrate. Thinking is a purely physical process. No one can tell us how to begin to think, all they can do is to tell us what happens when we do think. In the grey matter of the brain are multitudes of blood-vessels, distributed equally all over the brain, and when we think, the blood gathers to the one part of the brain we are using. This is called concentration. Dissipated thinking means that the blood goes back to the other parts of the brain and wakens up associated ideas. When we focus our will around certain thoughts, the blood converges to that particular part of the brain, and if we can hold our wills fixed there for five minutes, we have done a tremendous thing, we have begun to form the habit of mental concentration. The majority of us allow our brains to wool-gather, we never concentrate on any particular line. Concentration is physical, not spiritual. The brain must be brought into order by concentration, then when the Spirit of God brings a spontaneous illumination of a particular theme instantly the brain is at the disposal of God. If we have not learned to concentrate, the brain cannot focus itself anywhere, it fusses all round and wool-gathers. No one is responsible for that but ourselves.

This is true in ordinary thinking, and the same brain is used by the Holy Spirit. We have to learn to bring "every thought into captivity to the obedience of Christ"; to 'stay our imagination' on God. This can only be done by concentration, by fixing our thoughts and our imagination deliberately on God. The majority of us are unable

79

to fix our thoughts in prayer, we lie all abroad before God and do not rouse ourselves up to lay hold of Him, consequently we have wandering thoughts continually. God will not bring every thought and imagination into captivity; we have to do it, and that is the test of spiritual concentration. The inattentive, slovenly way we drift into the presence of God is an indication that we are not bothering to think about Him. Whenever our Lord spoke of prayer, He said, "*ask*." It is impossible to ask if you do not concentrate. The marvel of the goodness of God is that He does so much for us; if we would only meet with physical obedience what God does for us spiritually, the whole of our body would be under such control that we should apprehend His meaning when He speaks. It is not a question of learning a thing outside but of determination inside. God gives us the Holy Spirit not only for holy living but for holy thinking, and we are held responsible if we do not think concentratedly along the right lines. To concentrate with our mind fixed on one trend of things is never easy to begin with. There never is a time when we cannot begin to concentrate.

"Be ye not unwise, but understanding what the will of the Lord is." We have to use the same power of concentration spiritually as we do naturally. How are we going to find out the will of God? 'God will communicate it to us.' He will not. His will is there all the time, but we have to discover it by being renewed in our minds, by taking heed to His word and obeying it. If we are not going to be "conformed to this world; but . . . transformed," we must use our brains. God does the spiritual, powerful part we cannot do; but we have to work it out, and as we do the obeying we prove, i.e., 'make out,' "what is that good, and acceptable, and perfect, will of God."

We need to make our own nature the ally of the Spirit of God. The grace of God never fails us, but we often fail the grace of God because we do not practise. If we do not practise when there is no need, we shall never do it when there is a need. When people say, 'I cannot think, I have not the gift,' they mean that they have never used their brains. We all have bodies and brains. When we use our brains in concentration in a way we have never done before, we will have growing pains; a headache after thinking is a sign we have brains. The more we work and get beyond the conscious stage of doing things, the more easily will we do them. We all have unconscious mental methods. Never imitate to stick to what you imitate; imitate only in order to provoke your mind to know its own mechanism.

An artist is one who not only sees but is prepared to pay the price of acquiring the technical knowledge to express what he sees. An artistic person is one who has not enough art in him to make him work at the technique of art whereby he can express himself, he indulges in moods and tones and impressions; consequently there are more artistic people than there are artists. The same is true of poetry, there are many people with poetic notions, but very few poets. It is not enough for a man to feel the divine flame burning in him; unless he goes into the concentrated, slogging business of learning the technique of expression, his genius will be of no use to anyone. Apply these illustrations spiritually: if we have not enough of the life of God in us to overcome the difficulty of expressing it in our bodies, then we are living an impoverished spiritual life. Think of the illuminations the Spirit of God has given you; He expected you to bring your physical body which He made into obedience to the vision, and you never attempted to but let it drift, and when the crisis came and God looked for you to be His mouthpiece, you crumpled all to pieces. You had not formed the habit of apprehending; your physical machine was not under control. It is a terrible thing to sit down to anything.

Beware of being side-tracked by the idea that you can develop a spiritual life apart from physical accompaniments. It is a desperately dangerous thing to allow the spiritual vision to go ahead of physical obedience.

Do some practical obeying.

THE WAY OF APPRECIATION BY THE SOUL.

"be filled with the Spirit." (v. 18.)

What is Possible in the Way of Inspiration. There are two ways of inspiration possible—being drunk with wine, and being filled with the Spirit. We have no business to be nondescript, drunk neither one way nor the other. A man may be sober and incapable as well as drunk and incapable. Watch human nature; we are so built that if we do not get thrilled in the right way, we will get thrilled in the wrong. If we are without the thrill of communion with God, we will try to get thrilled by the devil, or by some concoction of human ingenuity. Don't be inspired with wine, the counterfeit of the Spirit, says Paul, but be filled with the Spirit. Enthusiasm is the idea—intoxicated with the life of God. Paul puts it as a command, 'Be being filled.' When our Lord talked to the woman of Samaria, He said, "the water that I shall give him shall be in him a well of water springing up into everlasting life." Profoundly speaking, there is no re-filling; "a well of water" is there all the time. The picture is not that of a channel, but of a fountain, a continual infilling and overflowing of the inspiration of God.

In the matter of inspiration the first thing to watch is the temper of our own soul. A blameworthy temper of mind about another soul will end in the spirit of the devil. We cannot approach God in a wrong temper of mind, it will put a shutter down between and we shall not see Him. God introduces us to people who conduct themselves to us as we have conducted ourselves to Him, and if we do not recognise what He is doing we will ride a moral hobby-horse—'I will not be treated like that.' There is no further inspiration possible from the Spirit of God until that temper of mind is gone. "Take heed to your spirit, that ye deal not treacherously." Our Lord always puts His finger unerringly on the thing that is wrong. *"First be reconciled . . ."* (Matthew v. 24). The next thing we have to watch is our private relationship with God. Are we determined to prove that God must do what we have said He must? If so, our intercession becomes frenzied fanaticism. Or are we only concerned about being brought into an understanding of God, which is the real meaning of prayer? The greatest barrier to intercession is that we take ourselves so seriously, and come to the conclusion that God is reserved with us; He is not. God has to ignore things we take so seriously until our relationship to Him is exactly that of a child. If we are watching the temper of our minds towards other people and towards God, there will be the continual incoming and outflowing of the inspiration of God, a fresh anointing of the Holy Spirit all the time. Imagine Jesus being jaded in the life of God! There was never anything jaded about Him. When we are jaded there is always a reason, and it is either the temper of our mind towards another or towards God. We have no business to be half-dead spiritually, to hang like clogs on God's plan; we should be filled with a radiant intensity of life, living at the highest pitch all the time without any reaction. "I am come that they might have life, and that they might have it more abundantly."

Be being filled with the life Jesus came to give.

WHAT TO THINK ABOUT

Philippians iv. 8.

Never run away with the idea that it does not matter much what we believe or think; it does. What we think and believe, we *are*; not what we say we think and believe, but what we really do think and believe, we are; there is no divorce at all. To believe, in the sense our Lord used the word, is never an intellectual act but a moral act. The following quotation from Dr. Arnold of Rugby explains the way fanatics are made, and also points out the incongruity of those Christians who are sanctified and yet show an unconscionable bigotry and narrow-mindedness in their mental outlook:—

"I am quite sure that it is a most solemn duty to cultivate our understandings to the uttermost, for I have seen the evil moral consequences of fanaticism to a greater degree than I ever expected to see them realised; and I am satisfied that a neglected intellect is far oftener the cause of mischief to a man than a perverted or over-valued one. Men retain their natural quickness and cleverness while their reason and judgment are allowed to go to ruin, and thus they do work their minds and gain influence, and are pleased at gaining it; but it is the undisciplined mind which they are exercising, instead of one wisely disciplined."

"whatsoever things are true, . . . think on these things."

It is more painful to think about these things than to think about what we know, about what is old in our experience, because immediately we begin to think God's thoughts after Him we have to bring concentration to bear, and that takes time and discipline. When once the mind begins to think, the horizon is continually broadening and widening, there is a general unsettlement, and the danger is to go back to the old confined way and become fanatical and obstinate. This explains why some people who really are God's children have such an inveterate dislike of study. They do not quite call it the devil, but they come pretty near it. To give time to soak in God's truth, time to find out how to think along God's line, appears to them a snare and delusion. All the insubordination and difficulties and upsets come from the people who will not think. 'Glean your thinking,' says Paul, and we must do it by will. What are we doing with our brains now that we have entered into the sanctified life? The Holy Spirit energises the will to a complete mastery of the brain; then don't be a wool-gatherer mentally. If we are saved and sanctified by God's grace, it is unadulterated mental laziness on our part not to rouse ourselves up to think. It is not a question of the opportunities of learning, but of the determination to be continually renewed in the spirit of our mind.

(a) *The Topic of the Things of Truth.* The things of truth are things which are in keeping with the Person of Truth, the Lord Jesus Christ: *"I am the Truth."* Truth therefore means not only accuracy, but accuracy about something that corresponds with God. We must distinguish between an accurate fact and a truthful fact. The devil, sin, disease, spiritualism, are all accurate facts, but they are not truthful facts. Christian Science makes the blunder of saying that because sin is not of the nature of truth, therefore it is not a fact. But sin is a fact. The accuracy of facts and the accuracy of the facts of truth are two different things. Never say that things that are not of the truth are non-existent. There are many facts that are not of the truth, that is, they do not correspond with God, Paul says, Limit your thinking to the things that are true.

Have you begun to discipline your mind in that way? If you have, people may pour bucket-loads of the devil's garbage over your head but it will have no more effect on you than dirt has on a crystal. Our minds are apt to be all abroad, like an octopus with its tentacles out to catch everything that comes along—newspaper garbage, spiritualistic garbage, advertisement garbage, we let them all come and make a dumping ground of our heads, and then sigh and mourn and say we cannot think right thoughts. Beware of saying you cannot help your thoughts; you can; you have all the almighty power of God to help you. We have to learn to bring every thought into captivity to the obedience of Christ, and it takes time. We want to reach it in a moment like a rocket, but it can only be done by a gradual moral discipline, and we do not like discipline, we want to do it all at once.

(b) *The Topic of the Things of Honesty*, 'honourable' (R.V.), 'reverend' (R.V. marg.). The word 'honest' has come down in the world, it means something noble and massive, awe-inspiring and grand, that awakens our reverence and inspires sublime thoughts, as a cathedral does. The things of honesty make a man's character sublime, and Paul counsels us to think on these things. See that there is a correspondence between a sublime piece of architecture and your character. Anything that awakens the sense of the sublime is an honourable thing. In the natural realm a sunset, a sunrise, mountain scenery, music, or poetry will awaken a sense of the sublime. In the moral world, truthfulness in action will awaken it. Truthfulness in action is different from truthfulness in speech. Truth-speaking people are an annoyance, they spank children for having imagination; they are sticklers for exact accuracy of speech and would have everyone say the same thing, like gramophone records; they drag down the meaning of truth out of its sphere. So we mean truthfulness in action, a true act all through.

Another thing that awakens the sense of the sublime is suffering that arises from the misunderstanding of those whom one esteems highest. Jesus Christ brought this suffering to the white heat of perfection; He let those He esteemed misunderstand Him foully and never once vindicated Himself, but was meek towards all His Father's dispensations for Him. That is moral sublimity. In the spiritual world, the sense of the sublime is awakened by such a life as that of Abraham, or of the Apostle Paul, or of anyone going through the trial of their faith. "Though He slay me, yet will I trust Him." That is the most sublime utterance of faith in the Old Testament.

We are accustomed to think of honourable things in connection with the spiritual world, but there are honourable things in the natural world and in the moral world as well. We have the idea that God has only to do with the spiritual, and if the devil can succeed in keeping us with that idea, he will have a great deal of his own way; but Paul pushes the battle-line into every domain— "*whatsoever* things are honest, . . . think on these things," because behind them all is God.

(c) *The Topic of the Things of Justice.* Justice means rightness with God; nothing is just until it is adjusted to God. The justice of a law court is superficial exactitude between man and man. That is why we often rebel against the verdict of a law court, although its justice can be proved to the hilt. Paul is not referring to justice between man and man, but to the very essence of justice, and he knows no justice where God is ignored. The great exhibition of justice is Jesus Christ; there was no superficial exactitude in His life because He was perfectly at one with God. The standard all through the Sermon on the Mount is that of conduct arising from a right relationship to God. We say—'Oh well, I certainly would show a forgiving spirit to them if they would be right with me.' Jesus said, 'If ye forgive not men their trespasses, neither will your Father forgive your trespasses." Take any of the teaching of the Sermon on the Mount and you will find it is never put on the ground that because a man is right with me, therefore I will be the same to him, but always on the ground of a right relationship to Jesus Christ first, and then the showing of that same relationship to others. To look for justice from other people is a sign of deflection from devotion to Jesus Christ. Never look for justice, but never cease to give it. We think of justice in the most absurd connections—because people tread on our little notions, our sense of what is right, we call that injustice. When once we realise how we have behaved towards God all the days of our life until we became adjusted to Him through the Atonement, our attitude to our fellow men will be that of absolute humility (cf. Ephesians iv. 32).

(d) The Topic of the Things of Purity. Purity is not innocence, it is much more. Purity means stainlessness, an unblemishedness that has stood the test. Purity is learned in private, never in public. Jesus Christ demands purity of mind and imagination, chastity of bodily and mental habits. The only men and women it is safe to trust are those who have been tried and have stood the test; purity is the outcome of conflict, not of necessity. You cannot trust innocence or natural goodness; you cannot trust possibilities. This explains Jesus Christ's attitude. Our Lord trusted no man (see John ii. 24–25), yet He was never suspicious, never bitter; His confidence in what God's grace could do for any man was so perfect that He never despaired of anyone. If our trust is placed in human beings, we will end in despairing of every one. But when we limit our thinking to the things of purity we shall think only of what God's grace has done in others, and put our confidence in that and in nothing else. Look back over your life and see how many times you have been pierced through with wounds, and all you can say when God deals with you is, 'Well, it serves me right; over and over again God taught me not to trust in myself, not to put confidence in men, and yet I have persisted in doing it.' God holds us responsible for being ignorant in these matters, and the cure for ignorance is to think along the lines Paul indicates here. It will mean that we shall never stand up for our own honour, or for the honour of others; we shall stand only for the honour and the dignity of the Lord Jesus Christ. Our temperamental outlook is altered by thinking; and when God alters the disposition, temperament begins to take its tone from the new disposition. These things are not done suddenly, they are only done gradually, by the stern discipline of the life under the teaching of the Spirit of God.

(e) *The Topic of the Things of Loveliness*, i.e., the things that are morally agreeable and pleasant. The word 'lovely' has the meaning of juicy and delicious. That is the definition given by Calvin, and he is supposed to be a moloch of severity! We have the idea that our duty must always be disagreeable, and we make any number of duties out of diseased sensibilities. If our duty is disagreeable, it is a sign that we are in a disjointed relationship to God. If God gave some people a fully sweet cup, they would go carefully into a churchyard and turn the cup upside down and empty it, and say, 'No, that could never be meant for me.' The idea has become incorporated into their make-up that their lot must always be miserable. Once we become rightly related to God, duty will never be a disagreeable thing of which we have to say with a sigh, 'Oh, well, I must do my duty.' Duty is the daughter of God. Never take your estimate of duty after a sleepless night, or after a dose of indigestion; take your sense of duty from the Spirit of God and the word of Jesus. There are people whose lives are diseased and twisted by a sense of duty which God never inspired; but once let them begin to think about the things of loveliness, and the healing forces that will come into their lives will be amazing. The very essence of godliness is in the things of loveliness; think about these things, says Paul.

(f) *The Topic of the Things of Good Report*, literally, the things that have a fine face, a winning and attractive tone about them. What should we be like after a year of thinking on these things? We might not be fatter, but I am certain we should look pleasanter! When we do think about the things of good report we shall be astonished to realise where they are to be found; they are found where we only expected to find the opposite. When our eyes are fixed on Jesus Christ we begin to see qualities blossoming in the lives of others that we never saw there before. We see people whom we have tabooed and put on the other side exhibiting qualities we have never exhibited, although we call ourselves saved and sanctified. Never look for other people to be holy; it is a cruel thing to do, it distorts your view of yourself and of others. Could anyone have had a sterner view of sin than Jesus had, and yet had anyone a more loving, tender patience with the worst of men than He had? The difference in the attitude is that Jesus Christ never expected men to be holy; He knew they could not be: *He came to make men holy.* All He asks of men is that they acknowledge they are not right, then He will do all the rest—"Blessed are the poor in spirit." It comes back to the central message of Jesus Christ, *"I, if I be lifted up. . . ."* If we preach anything other than "Jesus Christ, and Him crucified," we make our doctrines God and ourselves the judge of others. Think of the times we have hindered the Spirit of God by trying to help others when only God could help them, because we have forgotten to discipline our own minds. It is the familiar truth that we have to be stern in proclaiming God's word, let it come out in all its rugged bluntness, unwatered down and unrefined; but when we deal with others we have to remember that we are sinners saved by grace. The tendency to-day is to do exactly the opposite, we make all kinds of excuses for God's word—'Oh God does not expect us to be perfect,' and when we deal with people personally we are amazingly hard.

All these things lead us back to Jesus Christ—He is the Truth; He is the Honourable One; He is the Just One; He is the Pure One; He is the altogether Lovely One; He is the only One of Good Report. No matter where we start from, we will always come back to Jesus Christ.

THE FRONTIERS OF CHRISTIAN THINKING.

"if there be any virtue, and if there be any praise, think on these things."

Paul seems to come to the conclusion that he has not made the area of thinking wide enough yet, so he says, 'If there is any morally excellent thing, anything whatever to praise, anything recommendable, take account of it.'

We are apt to discard the virtues of those who do not know Jesus Christ and call them pagan virtues. Paul counsels, 'If there is any virtue anywhere in the world, think about it,' because the natural virtues are remnants of God's handiwork and will always lead to the one central Source, Jesus Christ. We have to form the habit of keeping our mental life on the line of the great and beautiful things Paul mentions. It is not a prescribed ground. It is we who make limitations and then blame God for them. Many of us behave like ostriches, we put our heads in the sand and forget altogether about the world outside—'I have had this and that experience and I am not going to think of anything else.' After a while we have aches and pains in the greater part of ourselves, which is outside our heads, and then we find that God sanctifies every bit of us, spirit, soul and body. God grant we may get out into the larger horizons of God's Book.

Always keep in contact with those books and those people that enlarge your horizon and make it possible for you to stretch yourself mentally. The Spirit of God is always the spirit of liberty; the spirit that is not of God is the spirit of bondage, the spirit of oppression and depression. The Spirit of God convicts vividly and tensely, but He is always the Spirit of liberty. God Who made the birds never made bird-cages; it is men who make bird-cages, and after a while we become cramped and can do nothing but chirp and stand on one leg. When we get out into God's great free life, we discover that that is the way God means us to live "the glorious liberty of the children of God."

THINKING GODLINESS

Philippians iv. 5–8 (R.V.); iii. 7–14.

In physical life we do best those things we have habitually learned to do, and the same is true in mental and spiritual life. We do not come into the world knowing how to do anything; all we do we have acquired by habit. Remember, habit is purely mechanical.

THINKING HABITS.

Philippians iv. 5.

Our thinking processes are largely subject to the law of habit. "Let your forbearance," i.e., self-control, "be made known unto all men." Self-control is nothing more than a mental habit which controls the body and mind by a dominant relationship, viz.: the immediate presence of the Lord—for "the Lord is at hand." The danger in spiritual matters is that we do not *think* godliness; we let ideas and conceptions of godliness lift us up at times, but we do not form the habit of godly thinking. Thinking godliness cannot be done in spurts, it is a steady habitual trend. God does not give us our physical habits or our mental habits; He gives us the power to form any kind of habits we like, and in the spiritual domain we have to form the habit of godly thinking.

To a child the universe is a great confusing, amazing 'outsideness'; when the child grows to be a man he has the same nervous system and brain, but the will has come in and determined his tendencies and impulses. It is natural for a child to be impulsive; but it is a disgraceful thing for a man or woman to be guided by impulse. To be a creature of impulse is the ruin of mental life. The one thing our Lord checked and disciplined in the disciples was impulse; the determining factor was to be their relationship to Himself.

We are so made that our physical life gives us an affinity with every material thing; our thinking life gives us affinity with everything in the mental realm, and it is the same with our moral and spiritual life. We are held responsible by God for the way we deal with the great mass of things that come into our lives. We all have susceptibilities in every direction; everyone is made in the same way as everyone else; consequently it is not true to say we cannot understand why some people like to devote themselves to pleasure, to races and dancing, etc. If we do not understand it, it is because part of our nature has become atrophied. Whatever one human being can do, either in the way of good or bad, any human being can do. There are things we must deny, but the negation that is the outcome of ignorance is of no value whatever to the character; the denial by will is of enormous value. "If thy right eye causeth thee to stumble, pluck it out and cast it from thee . . ." (Matthew v. 29, R.V.); determine to select those elements of your conscious life that are going to tell for the characteristic of godliness.

TRENDING HABITUALLY.

Philippians iv. 6.

We have to watch the trend of things. The trend of our conscious life is determined by us, not by God, and Paul makes the determining factor in the conscious life of a godly person the determination to pray. Prayer is not an emotion, not a sincere desire; prayer is the most stupendous effort of the will. "Let your requests be made known unto God. And the peace of God, which passeth all understanding, shall guard your hearts and your thoughts in Christ Jesus," the poising power of the peace of God will enable you to steer your course in the mix-up of ordinary life. We talk about 'circumstances over which we have no control.' None of us have control over our circumstances, but we are responsible for the way we pilot ourselves in the midst of things as they are. Two boats can sail in opposite directions in the same wind, according to the skill of the pilot. The pilot who conducts his vessel on to the rocks says he could not help it, the wind was in that direction; the one who took his vessel into the harbour had the same wind, but he knew how to trim his sails so that the wind conducted him in the direction he wanted. Never allow to yourself that you could not help this or that; and never say you reach anywhere *in spite of* circumstances; we all attain *because* of circumstances and no other way.

> "Let us not always say
> 'Spite of this flesh to-day
> I strove, made head, gained ground upon the whole!' "

TOUCHING HABITUAL FUNDAMENTS.

Philippians iv. 8.

There is a difference between thinking and grinding. Such subjects as languages or mathematics require grinding, and it is no use saying we have not the mental power to grind, we have; and the more we grind the more the mechanical part of our nature will come to our aid if we keep at it uninterruptedly. When it comes to matters of imagination, different faculties are needed. Some minds are more easily put on the grind than others, and some are more easily taught on the imaginative line than others. We have to discipline ourselves along both lines. Insubordination is another name for mental laziness. Watch the difference between listening to a language lesson and to a sermon or lecture; you will be worn out in no time by the former unless you have learned to grind; but with the latter, after a few sentences, your mind is kindled through the connection of previous thinking. It is not that we are gifted in this way but that we are created in this way. Paul insists on this very law . . . "whatsoever things are true, . . . *think* on these things." Glean your thinking; don't allow your mind to be a harbourage for every kind of vagabond sentiment; resolutely get into the way of disciplining your impulses and stray thinking. The law of attention controls the mind and keeps it from shifting hither and thither.

The forming of a new habit is difficult until you get into the way of doing the thing, then everything you meet with aids you in developing along the right line. It is good practice to sit down for five minutes and do nothing; in that way you will soon discover how little control you have over yourself. In forming a new habit it is vitally important to insist on bringing the body under control first. Paul says, 'I maul and master my body, in case, after preaching to other people, I am disqualified myself' (1 Corinthians ix. 27, Moffatt). The natural man is created by God as well as the new man in Christ, and the new man has to be manifested by the natural man in his mortal flesh. Paul puts it very practically in Romans vi. 19, 'Your members have been used to serve the disposition of sin; now that you are made free from sin, use your members to serve the disposition of righteousness.' In 1 Corinthians x. 31 (Moffatt) he puts it still more practically: "So whether you eat or drink, or whatever you do, let it be all done for the glory of God." It is difficult to begin with, but as you go on you find it becomes easier until you are able not only to practise the presence of God in your spirit, but are able to prove by the habits of your actual life that your body is the temple of the Holy Ghost.

NATIVE AND ACQUIRED INTERESTS.

Philippians iii. 7.

There are some subjects that are natively interesting, and other subjects for which we have to acquire an interest. A child's mind is only natively interested; an adult mind if it is well formed has voluntarily acquired an interest in other subjects. We imagine that a native interest will develop into an acquired interest all at once, but it won't. It will only become a dominant interest when it has come into the very make-up of our being. Think of the things you are interested in to-day, the things that are really forming your mind, you can remember the time when you had no affinity with them at all, they awakened no interest in you. What has happened? The Spirit of God by the engineering of God's Providence has brought some word of His and connected it with your circumstances in such a way that the whole of your outlook is altered. "The old things are passed away; behold, they are become new" (2 Corinthians v. 17, R.V.). *God alters the thing that matters.*

The interests of a child are altogether in the senses, and in teaching a child you must begin by interesting him. The teacher who succeeds best with children is the one who does things before them; it is no use teaching children abstract stuff. That is why it is necessary in teaching a young life, whether young in years of the flesh or the spirit, for a teacher to attend more to what he does than to what he says. The crystallising point of our Lord's teaching lies here, and the reason our Lord condemned the Pharisees was that "they say, and do not." Everyone has a perfect right to come and ask those of us who teach whether we practise what we teach. The influence of our teaching is in exact proportion to our practical doing.

In Philippians iii. 7–8, Paul states that he has flung overboard the things that were natively interesting to him in order to acquire other interests which at one time were of no value to him; and now the whole of his attention is set on Jesus Christ's idea for him, "I press on, if so be that I may apprehend, seeing that also I was apprehended" (Philippians iii. 12, R.V., marg.) A man can go through any drudgery under heaven to attain the object he has in view. Paul's object was to win Christ, and he counted "all things to be loss," and "suffered the loss of all things, counting them but refuse," to attain his object.

NURTURING APPRECIATION.

Philippians iii. 10.

These words never fail to awaken a thrill of emotion in the heart of every Christian, but the question arises—'How can I become interested in these matters to the degree that the Apostle was interested in them?' The only way in which a truth can become of vital interest to me is when I am brought into the place where that truth is needed. Paul calls the people to whom the gospel is not vitally interesting, 'dead'; but when once they are brought under conviction of sin, the one thing they will listen to is the thing they despised before, viz., the gospel. There is a difference between the way we try to appreciate the things of God and the way in which the Spirit of

God teaches. We begin by trying to get fundamental conceptions of the creation and the world; why the devil is allowed; why sin exists. When the Spirit of God comes in He does not begin by expounding any of these subjects; He begins by giving us a dose of the plague of our own heart; He begins where our vital interests lie—in the salvation of our souls. In every Christian life spiritual sentiment is at times carried to the white heat of devotion, but the point is how can we so attend to these things that the devotion is there all the time. In spiritual life most of us progress like frogs; we jump well at times, but at other times we stay a long while in one place until God in His Providence tumbles up our circumstances. The Apostle Paul's life was not a frog-jumping business, not a spasmodic life kept going by conventions and meetings, but an abiding, steadfast, attending life. If we are alive spiritually, the Spirit of God will continually prod us to attend to new phases of our salvation, and if we sit down, we sit on something that hurts. There will be always something that "bids nor sit nor stand but go!" The people who are of absolutely no use to God are those who have sat down and have become overgrown with spiritual mildew; all they can do is to refer to an experience they had twenty or thirty years ago. That is of no use whatever, we must be vitally at it all the time. With Paul it was never 'an experience I once had', but "*the life which I now live.*"

Negotiating Associations.

Philippians iii. 12–14.

We have to build up useful associations in our minds, to learn to associate things for ourselves, and it can only be done by determination. There are ideas associated in each of our minds that are not associated in the mind of anyone else, and this accounts for the difference in individuals. For instance, learn to associate the chair you sit in with nothing else but study; associate a selected secret place with nothing but prayer. We do not sufficiently realise the power we have to infect the places in which we live and work by our prevailing habits in those places.

The law of associated ideas applied spiritually means that we must drill our minds in godly connections. How many of us have learned to associate our summer holidays with God's Divine purposes? to associate the early dawn with the early dawn on the Sea of Galilee after the Resurrection? If we learn to associate ideas that are worthy of God with all that happens in Nature, our imagination will never be at the mercy of our impulses. Spiritually, it is not a different law that works, but the same law. When once we have become accustomed to connecting these things, every ordinary occurrence will serve to fructify our minds in godly thinking because we have developed our minds along the lines laid down by the Spirit of God. It is not done once for always; it is only done *always*. Never imagine that the difficulty of doing these things belongs peculiarly to you, it belongs to every one. The character of a person is nothing more than the habitual form of his associations.

Learn to beware of marginal pre-occupations that continually provoke other associations. For instance, there are people who cultivate the margin of vision; they look at you, but out of the margin of their eye they are really occupied with something else all the time; and in the mental realm there are people who never pay attention to the subject immediately in hand, but only to the marginal subjects round about. Spiritually there is the same danger. Jesus Christ wants us to come to the place where we see things from His standpoint and are identified with His interests only. "My one thought is, by forgetting what lies behind me and straining to what lies before me, to press on to the goal . . ." (Moffatt).

Concentration is the law of life mentally, morally and spiritually.

THE MIND OF CHRIST

Philippians ii. 5–8 (R.V.).

"Have this mind in you, which was also in Christ Jesus."

We are apt to forget that the mind of Christ is super-natural, His mind is not a human mind at all. Never run away with the idea that because you have the Spirit of Christ, therefore you have His mind. God gives us the Spirit of Jesus, but He does not give us His mind; we have to construct the mind of Christ, and it can only be done as we work out in the habits of a holy life the things that were familiar in the life of our Lord. We cannot form the mind of Christ once for always; we have to form it *always*; that is, all the time and in everything. "Acquire your soul," i.e., the new way of looking at things, "with patience" (Luke xxi. 19), and learn never to say fail! When God re-creates us in Christ Jesus He does not patch us up; He makes us *"a new creation."* Every power of our being is no longer to be used at the dictates of our right to ourselves, but to be subordinated to the Spirit of God in us Who will enable us to form the mind of Christ.

The type of mind Paul urges us to form is prescribed clearly—the mind of true humility; the mind "which was also in Christ Jesus" when He was on this earth, utterly self-effaced and self-emptied; not the mind of Christ when He was in glory. Humility is the exhibition of the Spirit of Jesus Christ, and is the touchstone of saintliness.

His Deity and our Dependence.

"Who, being originally in the form of God, counted it not a thing to be grasped to be on an equality with God." (Marg.)

Paul precludes the idea that Jesus thought nothing of Himself: our Lord thought truly of Himself. There was no assertion in any shape or form, and no presumption. It was along this line that Satan tempted Him—'Remember Who You are: You are the Son of God; then assert the prerogative of Sonship—command that these stones become bread; do something supernatural—cast Yourself down from hence . . .'

It was a temptation to the fulfilment of the Incarnation by a 'short cut.' Each time the temptation came, our Lord 'blunted' it: 'I did not come here to assert Myself; I came for God's will to be done through Me in His own way' (John vi. 38). Paul connects the two things—"on an equality with God": "not a thing to be grasped." Our Lord never once asserted His dignity, He never presumed on it.

When we are sanctified, the same temptation comes to us—'You are a child of God, saved and sanctified, presume on it, think it something to be grasped.' As long as our thought is fixed on our experience instead of on the God Who gave us the experience, the habit of making nothing of ourselves is an impossibility. If we think only along the line of our experience we become censorious, not humble. Sanctification is the gateway to a sanctified life, not to boasting about an experience. The habit of forming the mind of Christ will always make us obey our Lord and Master as He obeyed His Father, and there are whole domains of natural life to be brought under the control of this habit. It is not sinful to have a body and a natural life; if it were, it would be untrue to say that Jesus Christ was sinless, because He had a body and was placed in a natural life; but He continually sacrificed His natural life to the word and the will of His Father and made it a spiritual life, and we have to form the same habit. It is the discipline of a lifetime; we cannot do it all at once. We are absolutely dependent, and yet, strange to say, the last thing we learn spiritually is to make nothing of ourselves.

"*but emptied Himself*," Jesus Christ effaced the God-head in Himself so effectually that men without the Spirit of God despised Him. No one without the Spirit of God, or apart from a sudden revelation from God, ever saw the true Self of Jesus while He was on earth. He was "as a root out of a dry ground," thoroughly disadvantaged in the eyes of everyone not convicted of sin. The reference in 2 Corinthians viii. 9 is not to a wealthy *man* becoming poor, but to a wealthy *God* becoming poor for men. Our Lord is the time-representation of a Self-disglorified God. The purpose of the Incarnation was not to reveal the beauty and nobility of human nature, but in order to remove sin from human nature. To those who seek after wisdom the preaching of Christ crucified is foolishness; but when a man knows that his life is twisted, that the mainspring is wrong, he is in the state of heart and mind to understand why it was necessary for God to become Incarnate. The doctrine of the Self-limitation of Jesus is clear to our hearts first, not to our heads. We cannot form the mind of Christ unless we have His Spirit, nor can we understand our Lord's teaching apart from His Spirit. We cannot see through it; but when once we receive His Spirit we know implicitly what He means. Things which to the intellect may be hopelessly bewildering are lustrously clear to the heart of the humble saint (see Matthew xi. 25).

"*taking the form of a servant*," Our Lord took upon Him habitually the part of a slave: "I am among you as he that serveth"; consequently He could be 'put upon' to any extent, unless His Father prevented it (cf. John xix. 11); or His Father's honour was at stake (cf. Mark xi. 15–19). It was our Lord's right to be "in the form of God," but He renounced that right and took " the form of a bondservant" (marg.), not the form of a noble man, but of a slave. Our Lord crowned the words that the powers of this world detest—'servant,' 'obedience,' 'humility,' 'service.'

"*being made in the likeness of men*"; i.e. "the likeness of sinful flesh" (Romans viii. 3). The assimilation was as complete as our Lord's sinlessness would permit, and gave Him so truly human a life that by His fulfilling all righteousness in the face of temptation, He " condemned sin in the flesh."

"The nature was sinless in Him because He was sinless in it, not *vice versa*. . . . Jesus Christ does not stand for an originally holy human nature, but a sanctified or made-holy human nature." (*Du Bose.*)

The first Adam came in the flesh, not in sinful flesh: Jesus Christ, the last Adam, came on the plane of the first Adam; He partook of our nature but not of our sin. By His mighty Atonement He can lift us into the Kingdom in which He lived while He was on this earth so that we may be able to live a life freed from sin. That is the practical point the Apostle Paul is making.

"*and being found in fashion as a man, He humbled Himself, becoming obedient even unto death, yea, the death of the cross.*" Right at the threshold of His manhood our Lord took upon Him His vocation, which was to bear away the sin of the world—by *identification*, not by sympathy (John i. 29). Our Lord's object in becoming Deity Incarnate was to redeem mankind, and Satan's final onslaught in the Garden of Gethsemane was against our Lord *as Son of Man*, viz., that the purpose of His Incarnation would fail. The profundity of His agony has to do with the fulfilling of His destiny. The Cross is a triumph for *the Son of Man*; any and every man has freedom of access straight to the throne of God by right of what our Lord accomplished through His death on the Cross. *Though He was a Son*, He learned obedience *as a Saviour* by the things which He suffered, and thereby became the author of eternal salvation unto all them that obey Him.

"He was crucified through weakness." Jesus Christ represents God limiting His own power for one purpose: He died for the weak, for the ungodly, for sinners, and for no one else. "I came not to call the righteous, but sinners to repentance." No chain is stronger than its weakest link. In one aspect Jesus Christ became identified with the weakest thing in His own creation, a Baby; in another aspect He went to the depths of a bad man's hell, consequently from the babe to the vilest criminal Jesus Christ's substitution tells for salvation, nothing can prevail against Him.

The first thing the Spirit of God does in us is to efface the things we rely upon naturally. Paul argues this out in Philippians iii., he catalogues who he is and the things in which he might have confidence, 'but,' he says, 'I deliberately renounce all these things that I may gain Christ.' The continual demand to consecrate our gifts to God is the devil's counterfeit for sanctification. We have a way of saying—'What a wonderful power that man or woman would be in God's service.' Reasoning on man's broken virtues makes us fix on the wrong thing. The only way any man or woman can ever be of service to God is when he or she is willing to renounce all their natural excellencies and determine to be weak in Him— 'I am here for one thing only, for Jesus Christ to manifest Himself in me.' That is to be the steadfast habit of a Christian's life. Whenever we think we are of use to God, we hinder Him. We have to form the habit of letting God carry on His work through us without let or hindrance as He did through Jesus, and He will use us in ways He dare not let us see. We have to efface every other thought but that of Jesus Christ. It is not done once for all; we have to be always doing it. If once you have seen that Jesus Christ is All in all, make the habit of letting Him be All in all. It will mean that you not only have implicit faith that He is All in all, but that you go through the trial of your faith and prove that He is. After sanctification God delights to put us into places where He can make us wealthy. Jesus Christ counts as service not what we do for Him, but what we are to Him, and the inner secret of that is identity with Him in person. "*That I may know Him.*"

HIS DEDICATION AND OUR DISCIPLINE.

John xvii. 19.

"*And for their sakes I sanctify Myself.*"

How does that statement of our Lord fit in with our idea of sanctification? Sanctification must never be made synonymous with purification; Jesus Christ had no need of purification, and yet He used the word 'sanctify.' In the words, "I sanctify Myself," Jesus gives the key to the saint's life. Self is not sinful; if it were, how could Jesus say "I sanctify Myself"? Jesus Christ had no sin to deny, no wrong self to deny; He had only a holy Self. It was that Self He denied all the time, and it was that Self that Satan tried to make Him obey. What

could be holier than the will of the holy Son of God?
and yet all through He said, "not as I will, but as Thou
wilt." It was the denying of His holy Self that made
the marvellous beauty of our Lord's life.

If we have entered into the experience of sanctification,
what are we doing with our holy selves? Do we every
morning we waken thank God that we have a self to
give to Him, a self that He has purified and adjusted
and baptised with the Holy Ghost so that we might
sacrifice it to Him? Sacrifice in its essence is the exuber-
ant passionate love-gift of the best I have to the one I
love best. The best gift the Son of God had was His
Holy Manhood, and He gave that as a love-gift to God
that He might use it as an Atonement for the world.
He poured out His soul unto death, and that is to be
the characteristic of our lives. God is at perfect liberty
to waste us if He chooses. We are sanctified for one
purpose only, that we might sanctify our sanctification
and give it to God.

One of the dangers of present-day teaching is that it
makes us turn our eyes off Jesus Christ on to ourselves,
off the Source of our salvation on to salvation itself. The
effect of that is a morbid, hypersensitive life, totally
unlike our Lord's life, it has not the passion of abandon
that characterised Him. The New Testament never
allows for a moment the idea that continually crops up
in modern spiritual teaching—'I have to remember that
I am a specimen of what God can do.' That is inspired
by the devil, never by the Spirit of God. We are not
here to be specimens of what God can do, but to have our
life so hid with Christ in God that our Lord's words will
be true of us, that men beholding our good works will
glorify our Father in heaven. There was no 'show
business' in the life of the Son of God, and there is to be
no 'show business' in the life of the saint. Concentrate

on God, let Him engineer circumstances as He will, and wherever He places you He is binding up the broken-hearted through you, setting at liberty the captives through you, doing His mighty soul-saving work through you, as you keep rightly related to Him. Self-conscious service is killed, self-conscious devotion is gone, only one thing remains—"witnesses unto Me," Jesus Christ first, second and third.

"The Father abiding in Me doeth His works" (John xiv. 10, R.V.). Our Lord habitually submitted His will to His Father, that is, He engineered nothing but left room for God. The modern trend is dead against this sub-mission; we do engineer, and engineer with all the sanctified ingenuity we have, and when God suddenly bursts in in an expected way, we are taken unawares. It is easier to engineer things than determinedly to submit all our powers to God. We say we must do all we can: Jesus says we must let God do all He can.

"As the Father taught Me, I speak these things" (John viii. 28, R.V.). The secret of our Lord's holy speech was that He habitually submitted His intelligence to His Father. Whenever problems pressed on the human side, as they did in the temptation, our Lord had within Him-self the Divine remembrance that every problem had been solved in counsel with His Father before He became Incarnate (cf. Revelation xiii. 8), and that therefore the one thing for Him was to do the will of His Father, and to do it in His Father's way. Satan tried to hasten Him, tried to make Him face the problems as a Man and do God's will in His own way: "The Son can do nothing of Himself, but what He seeth the Father doing" (John v. 19, R.V.).

Are we intellectually insubordinate, spiritually stiff-necked, dictating to God in pious phraseology what we intend to let Him make us, hunting through the Bible to back up our pet theories? Or have we learned the secret of submitting our intelligence and our reasoning to Jesus Christ's word and will as He submitted His mind to His Father?

The danger with us is that we will only submit our minds to New Testament teaching where the light of our experience shines. "If we walk in the light"—as our experience is in the light? No, "if we walk in the light *as He is in the light* . . ." We have to keep in the light that God is in, not in the rays of the light of our experience. There are phases of God's truth that cannot be experienced, and as long as we stay in the narrow grooves of our experience we shall never become God-like, but specialists of certain doctrines—Christian oddities. We have to be specialists in devotion to Jesus Christ and in nothing else. If we want to know Jesus Christ's idea of a saint and to find out what holiness means, we must not only read pamphlets about sanctification, we must face ourselves with Jesus Christ, and as we do so He will make us face ourselves with God. "Be ye therefore perfect, even as your Father which is in heaven is perfect." When once the truth lays hold of us that we have to be God-like, it is the death-blow for ever to attempting things in our own strength. The reason we do attempt things in our own strength is that we have never had the vision of what Jesus Christ wants us to be. We have to be God-like, not good men and women. There are any number of good men and women who are not Christians.

The life of sanctification, of service, and of sacrifice, is the threefold working out in our bodies of the life of Jesus until the supernatural life is the only life. These are truths that cannot be *learned*; they can only be habitually *lived*.

OUR LORD ON HOW TO THINK

Matthew vi. 19–24.

We so readily look upon our Lord as Saviour in the fundamental way that we are apt to forget He is much more than Saviour, He is Teacher as well. In the same way we are familiar with the fact that all Christians have the Spirit of Christ, but not all Christians have the mind of Christ. We baulk this because we do not care to go into the laboriousness of forming His mind. We all have times of inspiration and ecstasy, but in these verses our Lord is not talking of times of ecstasy, but of the deliberate set of the life all through. God does His great sovereign works of grace in us and He expects us to bring all the powers under our control into harmony with what He has done. It is an arduous and difficult task, it is not done easily; and remember, God does not do it for us. We have to transform into real thinking possession for ourselves all that the Spirit of God puts into our spirits. The last reach of spirituality is the thinking power, i.e., the power to express what moves our spirit.

The Depository of Thought.

"Lay not up for yourselves treasures upon the earth . . . but lay up for yourselves treasures in heaven . . ." (vv. 19–21).

We have to lay up treasure for ourselves, it is not laid

up for us; and we have to lay it up in heaven, not on earth. To begin with, we do lay up the treasure of Jesus Christ's salvation on earth, we lay it up in our bodily lives, in our circumstances; and the curse spiritually is to lay up treasure in experience. Whatever we possess in the way of treasure on earth is liable to be consumed by moth and rust. Our Lord's counsel is to lay up treasure that never can be touched, and the place where it is laid up cannot be touched. "And made us to sit with Him in the heavenly places, in Christ Jesus" (Ephesians ii. 6, R.V.). No moth nor rust in the heavenly places, no possibility of thieves breaking through there. When we lay up treasure on earth it may go at any moment, but when we learn to lay up treasure in heaven, nothing can touch it—"therefore will not we fear, though the earth be removed, . . ."; it is perfectly secure.

Our Lord kept all His treasure of heart and mind and spirit in His oneness with the Father; He laid up treasure in heaven, not on earth. Our Lord never possessed anything for Himself (cf. 2 Corinthians viii. 9). The temptation of Satan was to get Him to lay up things in the earthly treasury, viz., in His own body, and to draw from that source: 'You are the Son of God, command these stones to be made bread; cast Yourself down and Your Father will send His angels to take care of you.' Our Lord never drew power from Himself, He drew it always from without Himself, that is, from His Father. "The Son can do nothing of Himself, but what He seeth the Father do" (John v. 19). The one great interest in our Lord's life was God, and He was never deflected from that centre by other considerations, not even by the devil himself, however subtly he came. "I and my Father are one." It was a oneness not of union, but of identity. It was impossible to distinguish between the Father and the Son, and the same is to be true of the saint and the Saviour: "that they may be one, even as We are one."

Examine your own experience as a saint and see where your treasure is: is it in the Lord, or in His blessings? In the degree that we possess anything for ourselves we are separated from Jesus. So many of us are caught up in the shows of things, not in the way of property and possessions, but of blessings, and all our efforts to persuade ourselves that our treasure is in heaven is a sure sign that it is not. If our treasure is in heaven we do not need to persuade ourselves that it is, we prove it is by the way we deal with matters of earth. The religion of Jesus Christ is a religion of personal relationship to God and has nothing to do with possessions. A sense of possessions is sufficient to render us spiritually dense because what we possess often possesses us. Whenever our Lord spoke of "life" He meant the kind of life He lived, and He says, "ye have not (this) life in yourselves" (John vi. 53, R.V.). Are we living the kind of life Jesus lived, with the skylights always open towards God, the windows of the ground floor open towards men, and the trap-door open towards sin and Satan and hell? Nothing was hidden from Jesus, all was faced with fearless courage because of His oneness with the Father.

"For where your treasure is, there will your heart be also." The Bible term "heart" is best understood if we simply say 'me,' it is the central citadel of a man's personality. The heart is the altar of which the physical body is the outer court, and whatever is offered on the altar of the heart will tell ultimately through the extremities of the body. "Keep thy heart with all diligence; for out of it are the issues of life."

Where do we make our depository of thinking? What do we brood on most, the blessings of God, or God

Himself? Look back over your life as a saint and you will see how the weaning has gone on from the blessing to the Blesser, from sanctification to the Sanctifier. When we no longer seek God for His blessings, we have time to seek Him for Himself.

The Division of Thinking.

"The lamp of the body is the eye: if therefore thine eye be single, thy whole body shall be full of light. . ." (*vv.* 22–23, R.V.).

The eye records exactly what it looks at, and conscience may be called the eye of the soul. A 'single eye' is essential to correct understanding spiritually. If the spirit is illumined by a conscience which has been rightly adjusted, then, says Jesus, the whole body is full of light because body, soul and spirit are united in a single identity with Himself. Beware of mistaking domination for identity. Identity is a oneness between two distinct persons in which neither person dominates, but the oneness dominates both. The only way this can be realised is along the line of our Lord's own life. Jesus Christ's first obedience was to the will of His Father, and our first obedience is to be to Him. The thing that detects where we live spiritually is the word 'obey.' The natural heart of man hates the word, and that hatred is the essence of the disposition that will not let Jesus Christ rule. The characteristic of our Lord's life was submission to His Father, not the crushing down of His own will to His Father's, but the love-agreement of His will with His Father's—'I am here for one thing only, to do Thy will, and I delight to do it.' When the Holy Spirit comes into us, the first thing He does is to make us men and women with a single motive, a 'single eye' for the glory of God. The essential element in the life of a saint is simplicity—"thy whole body shall be full of light."

But if thine eye be evil, thy whole body shall be full of darkness." What is an evil eye? Thinking that springs from our own point of view. "Is thine eye evil, because I am good?" (Matthew xx. 15). Jesus says that if our eye is evil, we shall misjudge what He does. If our spirits are untouched by God's Spirit, unillumined by God, the very light we have will become darkness. The disposition of the natural man, my claim to my right to myself, banks on things of which our Lord makes nothing, e.g., possessions, rights, self-realisation; and if that disposition rules, it will cause the whole body to be full of darkness. Darkness in this connection is our own point of view; light is God's point of view (cf. 1 John i. 7).

We deal much too lightly with sin; we deal with sin only in its gross actual form and rarely deal with it in its possessing form. "Howbeit, I had not known sin, except through the law: for I had not known coveting, except the law had said, Thou shalt not covet" (Romans vii. 7, R.V.). This inheritance of covetousness is the very essence of sin, and the only thing that can touch it is the Atonement of our Lord Jesus Christ. It is an aspect of sin which is not familiar to us. We must never lay the flattering unction to our souls that because we are not covetous of money or worldly possessions, we are not covetous of anything. Whatever we possess for ourselves is of the nature of sin. The fuss and distress of owning anything is the last remnant of the disposition of sin; whatever we own as Christians apart from Jesus Christ is a chance for the devil.

THE DECISIONS OF THE THINKER.

"No man can serve two masters: . . . Ye cannot serve God and mammon" (v. 24).

Have we allowed these inexorable decisions of our

Lord to have their powerful way in our thinking? The line of detachment runs all through our Lord's teaching: You cannot be good and bad at the same time; you cannot serve God and make your own out of the service; you cannot make 'honesty is the best policy' a motive, because immediately you do, you cease to be honest. There is to be only one consideration, a right relationship with God, and we must see that that relationship is never dimmed. Never compromise with the spirit of mammon. It is easy to associate mammon only with sordid things; mammon is the system of civilised life which organises itself without any consideration of God (cf. Luke xvi. 15).

To be detached from our possessions is the greatest evidence that we are beginning to form the mind of Christ. If it is possible to conceive being caused sore distress through the withdrawal of any particular form of blessing, it is a sure sign that we are still trying to serve two masters. For instance, can we say, not with our lips, but with our whole souls, "For I could wish that myself were accursed from Christ for my brethren"? Have we for one second got hold of the spirit that was in Paul when he said that, the very spirit of Jesus? Neither fear of hell nor hope of heaven has anything to do with our personal relationship to Jesus Christ, it is a life hid with Christ in God, stripped of all possessions saving the knowledge of Him. The great lodestar of the life is Jesus Himself, not anything He does for us.

This kind of thinking is impossible until we are spiritual, and when we become spiritual we realise how completely our thinking has been reconstructed. Watch God's method of teaching us to think along the lines He has taken our spirits by His grace. In the initial stages we learn that we cannot serve two masters by recognising the disposition that Paul calls "the carnal mind," and are only too passionately grateful to come to the place where we know that that disposition is identified with the death of Jesus (Romans vi. 6). No wonder Paul says "the carnal mind is enmity against God"; he does not say it is 'at enmity,' it *is* enmity against God. The carnal mind is the brother of the devil; he is all right until you bring him in contact with Jesus, but immediately you do he is a chip of the old block, he hates with an intense vehemence everything to do with Jesus Christ and His Spirit. 'My right to myself' is the carnal mind in essence, and we need a clear thinking view of what it means to be delivered from this disposition. It means that just as our personality used to exhibit a ruling disposition identical with the prince of this world, so the same personality can now exhibit an identity with the Lord Jesus Christ. Sanctification means that and nothing less. Sanctification is not *once for all*, but *once for always*. Sanctification is an instantaneous, continuous work of grace. If we think of sanctification as an experience once for all, there is an element of finality about it; we begin the hop, skip and jump testimony, 'Bless God, I am saved and sanctified,' and from that second we begin to get '*scantified*.' Sanctification means we have the glorious opportunity of proving daily, hourly, momentarily, this identity with Jesus Christ, and the life bears an unmistakable likeness to Him. The religion of Jesus Christ makes a man united, we are never meant to develop one part of our being at the cost of another part. When we are united with Jesus He garrisons every part, "and that wicked one toucheth him not."

Another way by which we learn that we cannot serve two masters is by putting away the aim of successful service for ever. When the seventy returned with joy, our Lord said, in effect, 'Don't rejoice that the devils are subject unto you, that is My authority through you; but rejoice that you are rightly related to Me.' It is sadly true that after an experience of sanctification many do try and serve two masters, they go into the joy of successful service, and slowly the eye becomes fixed on the sanctified 'show business' instead of on Jesus Himself. The only illustrations our Lord used of service were those of the vine (John xv. 1–6), and the rivers of living water (John vii. 37–39). It is inconceivable to think of the vine delighting in its own grapes; all that the vine is conscious of is the husbandman's pruning knife. All that the one out of whom rivers of living water are flowing is conscious of is belief in Jesus, and maintaining a right relationship to Him. Are we bringing forth fruit? We certainly are if we are identified with the Lord, luscious bunches of grapes for the Husbandman to do what He likes with. Pay attention to the Source, believe in Jesus, and God will look after the outflow. God grant we may let the Holy Ghost work out His passion for souls through us. We have not to imitate Jesus by having a passion for souls like His, but to let the Holy Ghost so identify us with Jesus that His mind is expressed through us as He expressed the mind of God.

Do we recognise Jesus Christ as our Teacher, or are we being led by vague spiritual impulses of our own? We have to learn to bring into captivity every thought to the obedience of Christ, and never be intellectually insubordinate. The teaching of Jesus Christ fits every point of a saint's life, but no point of the life of a natural man. If we apply these statements—"Seek ye first the kingdom of God and His righteousness . . ." "Take no thought for your life . . ."—to the life of a natural man, they are open to ridicule. We reverse God's order when we put Jesus as a Teacher first instead of Saviour; but when we are rightly related to God on the basis of the Atonement and begin to put Jesus Christ's teaching into practice, the marvel of marvels is we find it can be worked out.

If we as saints are strenuously seeking first the kingdom of God and His righteousness, His 'in-the-rightness,' all the time, we shall find not only the Divine un-reason of things, but the Divine reason of things working out beyond all our calculations—"and all these things shall be added unto you"; "for your heavenly Father knoweth that ye have need of all these things."

Never allow anything to fuss your relationship to Jesus Christ, neither Christian work, nor Christian blessing, nor Christian anything. Jesus Christ first, second and third; and God Himself by the great indwelling power of the Spirit within will meet the strenuous effort on your part, and slowly and surely you will form the mind of Christ and become one with Him as He was one with the Father. The practical test is—'Is Jesus Christ being manifested in my bodily life?'

EDUCATION IN HOLY HABIT

Psalm lxxxvi. 11; cxliii. 10.

Educative Evangelism *versus* Emotional Evangelism.

After a great crisis, such as an experience of salvation or sanctification, the danger is that we fix ourselves there and become spiritual prigs. A spiritual prig is one who has had an experience from God and has closed down on it, there is no further progress, no manifestation of the graces of the Spirit. The world pours contempt on that kind of Christian; they seem to have very little conscience, no judgment, and little will. We have to remember that unless we are energised by the Spirit of God, the margins of our spirits retain the damage done by the Fall.

By the Fall man not only died from God but fell into disunion with himself; that means it became possible for man to live in one of the three parts of his nature. What happens at new birth is that a man is not only introduced into a relationship to God, but into union with himself. The one thing that is essential to the new life is obedience to the Spirit of God Who energises our spirits, and that obedience must be complete in body, soul and spirit. It is not done suddenly. Salvation is sudden, but the working of it out in our lives is never sudden. It is moment by moment, here a little and there a little. God educates us down to the scruple. The area of our conscious life gradually gets broader and broader, and we begin to bring into line with the new life things we never thought of before.

We have to remember that we have a bodily machine which we must regulate, God does not regulate it for us. Until we learn to bring the bodily machine into harmony with God's Will, there will be friction, and the friction is a warning that part of the machine is not in working order. As we bring our bodily life into line bit by bit we shall find that we have God's marvellous grace on the inside enabling us to work out what He has worked in.

THE HABIT OF A REFINED CONSCIENCE.

Psalm lxxxvi. 11.

"Teach me Thy way, O Lord."

Conscience is that power in a man's soul that fixes on what he regards as the highest. Never call conscience the voice of God. If it were, it would be the most contradictory voice man ever listened to. For instance, Saul of Tarsus obeyed his conscience when he hounded men and women to death for worshipping Jesus Christ, and he also obeyed his conscience when later on in his life he acted in exactly the opposite way (see John xvi. 2; Acts xxvi. 9).

(a) Regulated after Sin. 1 Timothy i. 12–15.

After the disposition of sin is removed there is the need for conscience to be regulated. The Spirit of God always begins by repairing the damage after sin. The Apostle Paul argues in Romans vi, 'You did use your members as servants of the wrong disposition, now use them as servants of the right disposition.' It is a long way to go and many of us faint in the way. After a great spiritual crisis a man's conscience looks out towards God in a new light, the light which Jesus Christ throws upon God, and he has to walk in that light and bring his bodily life into harmony with what his conscience records.

Sin is the disposition of my right to myself, and it is also independence of God. These two aspects of sin are strikingly brought out in the Bible. Sin has to be dealt with from the ethical and intellectual aspect as well as from the spiritual aspect. The way sin works in connection with the life of the soul is in independence of God. Many people are never guilty of gross sins, they are not brought up in that way, they are too refined, have too much good taste; but that does not mean that the disposition to sin is not there. The essence of sin is my claim to my right to myself. I may prefer to live morally because it is better for me: I am responsible to no one, my conscience is my god. That is the very essence of sin. The true characteristic of sin is seen when we compare ourselves with Jesus Christ. We may feel quite happy and contented as long as we compare ourselves with other people, because we are all pretty much the same; but when we stand before Jesus Christ we realise what He meant when He said, "If I had not come . . . they had not had sin: . . . but now they have no cloke for their sin."

There is a difference between a refined conscience towards God and the fussy conscience of a hyper-conscientious person without the Spirit of God. Hyper-conscientious people are an absolute plague to live with, they are morally and spiritually nervous, always in terror expecting something to happen, always expecting trials, and they always come. Jesus Christ was never morally or spiritually nervous any more than He was physically nervous. The refinement of conscience in a Christian means learning to walk in accordance with the life of the Lord Jesus, drawing from God as He did. It is a life of absolute largeness and freedom.

(b) *Restored after Prejudice.* Acts xxvi. 4, 5.

Prejudice means a foreclosed judgment without

sufficiently weighing the evidence. When first we get right with God we are all prejudiced, ugly and distorted. When we come up against a prejudice we are stubborn and obstinate, and God leaves us alone; then the prejudice comes up again, and God waits, until at last we say 'I see,' and we learn how to be restored after our prejudices. Wherever there is a prejudice, the grace of God is hammering at it to break it down. The havoc in lives that are going on with God is accounted for because they are being restored after prejudice. Wherever you find a prejudice in yourself, take it to Jesus Christ. Our Lord is the only standard for prejudice, as He is the only standard for sin. Our Lord never worked from prejudice, never foreclosed His judgment without weighing the evidence. Are we letting God restore us after prejudice, or are we tied up in compartments? 'I have always worshipped God in this way and I always intend to.' Be careful! 'I have always believed this and that, and I always shall.' Be careful!

It is easier to be true to convictions formed in a vivid religious experience than to be true to Jesus Christ, because if we are going true to Jesus Christ our convictions have to be altered. Unless our experiences lead us on to a life, they will turn us into fossils; we will become mummified gramophones of convictions instead of "witnesses unto Me." Some of us are no good unless we are placed in the circumstances in which our convictions were formed; but God continually stirs up our circumstances and flings us out to make us know that the only simplicity is not the simplicity of a logical belief, but of a maintained relationship with Jesus Christ, and that is never altered in any circumstances. We must keep in unbroken touch with God by faith, and see that we give other souls the same freedom and liberty that God gives us. The duty of every Christian, and it is the last lesson we learn, is to make room for God to deal with other people direct; we will try and limit others and make them into our mould.

(c) *Roused after Compromise.* 1 Thessalonians ii. 10–12.

In the temptation of our Lord the compromise for good ends is pictured, 'Don't be so stern against sin; compromise judiciously with evil and You will easily win Your Kingship of men.' When we become rightly related to God our intellect is apt to say exactly the same thing, 'Don't be narrow; don't be so pronounced against worldliness, you will upset your friends.' Well, upset them, but never upset the main thing that God is after. There is always the tendency to compromise and we have to be roused up to recognize it. We have to walk in very narrow paths before God can trust us to walk in the wide ones. We have to be limited before we can be un-limited.

The Bible nowhere teaches us to be uncompromising in our opinions. Jesus did not say, 'Leap for joy when men separate you from their company for the sake of your convictions;' He said, 'Leap for joy when men cast out your name as evil, *for the Son of Man's sake.*' I may be such a pig-headed cross-patch, and have such determined notions of my own, that no one can live with me. That is not suffering for the Son of Man's sake, it is suffering for my own sake. Never compromise with anything that would detract from the honour of the Lord. Remember that the honour of Jesus is at stake in your bodily life and rouse yourself up to act accordingly.

THE HABIT OF RELIABLE JUDGMENT.

Psalm cxliii. 10.

"Teach me to do Thy will."

Our conscience may be right towards God, and yet we

may err in judgment. When the disposition has been perfectly adjusted towards God, it does not mean we have a perfectly adjusted body and brain; we have the same body and brain as before and we have to bring them into line until we form the judgment that is according to Jesus Christ. Many of us are impulsive spiritually and we live to be sorry for it. We have to form the habit of reliable judgment. God never gives us reliable judgment; He gives us a disposition which leads to a perfect judgment if we will work out that disposition.

(a) *The Disciplined Imagination.* 2 Corinthians x. 5.

We have to practise the submitting of our intelligence to Jesus Christ in His word. The imagination of a saint too often is vague and intractable. We have to learn to bring every thought and imagination into captivity to the obedience of Christ. An undisciplined imagination will destroy reliable judgment more quickly even than sin. Mental and spiritual insubordination is the mark of to-day. Jesus Christ submitted His intelligence to His Father. Do I submit my intelligence to Jesus Christ and His word?

(b) *The Illuminated Judgment.* 1 Corinthians iv. 5.

We have to learn to see things from Jesus Christ's standpoint. Our judgment is warped in every particular in which we do not allow it to be illuminated by Jesus Christ. For instance, if we listen to what our Lord says about money we shall see how we disbelieve Him. We quietly ignore all He says, He is so unpractical, so utterly stupid from the modern standpoint. "Seek ye first the kingdom of God and His righteousness; and all these things shall be added unto you." Which one of us believes that? If we are the children of God He will bring us into circumstances where we will be tested on every line to see whether we will form the habit of reliable judgment.

We have to learn to see things from Jesus Christ's

standpoint. He says, "All power is given unto Me . . ." The illumination of judgment comes personally when we recognise that the evil and wrong in our sphere of life is there not by accident, but in order that the power of God may come in contact with it as His power has come into us. When we come into contact with objectionable people the first natural impulse of the heart is to ask God to save them because they are a trial to us; He will never do it for that reason. But when we come to see those lives from Jesus Christ's standpoint and realise that He loves them as He loves us, we have a different relationship to them, and God can have His way in their lives in answer to our prayer.

(c) *The Resourcefulness of Tact.* 1 Corinthians ix. 19–23.

It is instructive to notice the way our Lord dealt with different people. In every case where He did not find bigotry He won them straight away. When we first become rightly related to God we have the idea that we have to talk to everyone, until we get one or two well deserved snubs; then our Lord takes us aside and teaches us His way of dealing with them. How impatient we are in dealing with others! Our attitude implies that we think God is asleep. When we begin to reason and work in God's way, He reminds us first of all how long it took Him to get us where we are, and we realise His amazing patience and we learn to come on other lives from above. As we learn to rely on the Spirit of God He gives us the resourcefulness of Jesus.

THE HABIT OF A RECTIFIED WILL.

Psalm lxxxvi. 11.

"unite my heart to fear Thy name."

Never look upon the will as something you possess as you do a watch. Will is the whole man active. Education in holy habit is along this line: at first we pray

"Teach me Thy way, O Lord;" then we pray, "Teach me to do Thy will," and step by step God teaches us what is His will; then comes a great burst of joy, 'I delight to do Thy will! There is nothing on earth I delight in more than in Thy will.' When we become rightly related to God we *are* the will of God in disposition, and we have to work out God's will; it is the freest, most natural life imaginable. Worldly people imagine that the saints must find it difficult to live with so many restrictions, but the bondage is with the world, not with the saints. There is no such thing as freedom in the world, and the higher we go in the social life the more bondage there is. True liberty exists only where the soul has the holy scorn of the Holy Ghost—I will bow my neck to no yoke but the yoke of the Lord Jesus Christ; there is only one law, and that is the law of God.

(a) *The Joy of Jesus.* John xv. 11.

The joy of Jesus lay in knowing that every power of His nature was in such harmony with His Father that He did His Father's will with delight. Some of us are slow to do God's will; we do it as if our shoes were iron and lead; we do it with a great sigh and with the corners of our mouths down, as if His will were the most arduous thing on earth. But when our wills are rectified and brought into harmony with God, it is a delight, a superabounding joy, to do God's will. Talk to a saint about suffering and he looks at you in amazement—'Suffering? Where does it come in?' It comes in on God's side along the line of interpretation; on the side of the saint it is an overwhelming delight in God; not delight in suffering, but if God's will should lead through suffering, there is delight in His will.

(b) *The Bent of Obedience.* John xv. 14.

Each one of us has to rule, to exercise some authority. When we have learned the obedience to God which was manifested in our Lord, we shall govern the world. Self-chosen authority is an impertinence. Jesus said that the great ones in this world exercise authority but that in His Kingdom it is not so; no one exercises authority over another because in His Kingdom the King is Servant of all (see Luke xxii. 24–27). If a saint tries to exercise authority it is a proof that he is not rightly related to Jesus Christ. The characteristic of a saint's life is this bent of obedience, no notion of authority anywhere about it. If we begin to say 'I have been put in this position and I have to exercise authority,' God will soon remove us. When there is steadfast obedience to Jesus, it is the authority of God that comes through and other souls obey at once.

(c) The Stage of Rare Fruition. John xv. 5, 8.

These verses refer to the stage of fruition—bringing forth fruit and the fruit remaining, that is what glorifies God and blesses others. If we as preachers or teachers are rightly related to God in obedience, God is continually pouring through us. When we stop obeying Him, everything becomes as hard and dry as a ditch in midsummer. When we are placed in a position by God and we keep rightly related to Him, He will see to the supply. Personally, whenever there is dryness I know that it is because I am forgetting some particular point in relation to my own life with God; when that is put right the flow is unhindered, and I believe this is true in every phase of work for God. If you are called to preach, preach; if you are called to teach, teach. Keep obedient to God on that line. The proof that you are on God's line is that other people never credit you with what comes through you. Jesus said, "Let your light so shine before men, that they may see your good works, and glorify your Father which is in heaven." Go on doing God's will, and you will be recreated while you do it.